Zen Gardens and Temples of
KYOTO

A Guide to Kyoto's Most Important Sites

John Dougill

Photography by John Einarsen

TUTTLE Publishing

Tokyo | Rutland, Vermont | Singapore

contents

PART ONE

Zen and Japanese Culture

Author's Note
Names are written in Japanese fashion (family name before given name), except for contemporary and modern figures who are referred to in the Western style.

Right Baisao, the legendary Edo-era tea seller, was a poet and Obaku monk who is enshrined at Manpuku-ji. Painting by Ito Jakuchu.
Inside front cover Sanmon gate, Nanzen-ji.
Inside back cover Round 'Window of enlightenment', Genko-an.
Page 1 A contemporary *shakuhachi* flute player.
Pages 2–3 View of the garden at Shisendo.

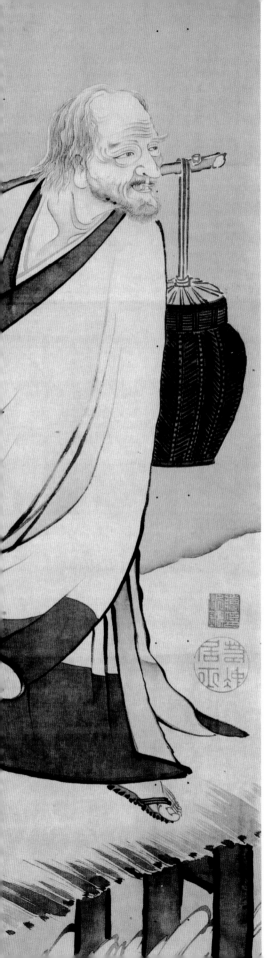

PART TWO

Kyoto's Zen Temples (In chronological order)

Zen in Kyoto

Each year I receive around 5,000 visitors to my temple who want to learn about Zen. They come from many different nationalities and backgrounds, ranging from businessmen to travelers and university students. Many have misconceptions about Zen, but nearly all are interested in developing and practicing 'mindfulness' in their lives.

Over the centuries, the Zen world in Kyoto has developed a unique culture in terms of focussing attention. It is evident in such 'Zen arts' as the tea ceremony and Chinese ink work. Its influence can be seen also in architecture, garden design, Japanese archery and martial arts. We can, in fact, find this clear, concentrated attention reflected in all aspects of Zen culture.

Luckily, we now have a book to guide us around the gardens and temples, revealing more than is immediately obvious. Between them, long-time residents of the city, John Dougill and John Einarsen, are able to bring the places to life. Author of an acclaimed cultural history of Kyoto, Dougill provides us with background information necessary to an understanding of the institutions. Award-winning John Einarsen's pictures balance panoramic views with eye-catching details to recreate the serenity and beauty of the Zen atmosphere.

It gives me great pleasure to recommend this book. It will help me communicate the rich experience of Zen to others as well as be a worthy souvenir for anyone visiting the city. And for those who have yet to experience Kyoto and its Zen heritage, the book will surely be a great enticement.

—*Reverend Takafumi Kawakami, Shunko-in Temple, Kyoto*

Right Dry landscape gardens use raked gravel to represent water, with rocks representing islands or mountains. Some see this in abstract terms as the movement of the mind interrupted by thought. For onlookers the garden may serve as an aid to meditation, while for monks raking the gravel is an exercise in mindfulness.

A National Treasure:
Kyoto and the Art of Zen

Kyoto is a city blessed in so many ways. It is home to seventeen World Heritage Sites. It is the city of Noh theater, ikebana and the tea ceremony; of gardens, geisha and Genji; of crafts, kimono and weaving; of poets, artists and aesthetes; of tofu, saké and *kaiseki* delicacies. It is also a city of temples, shrines and museums and of festivals and seasonal delights. And on top of all that, it is a city of Zen—Rinzai Zen, to be precise. It was here that the fusion of Chinese Chan with Japanese culture took place, producing a sect that has become synonymous with *satori*, or 'awakening'. Zen and Kyoto go together like love and Paris.

The genius of Japan, it is often said, is in the adoption and adaptation of foreign customs. Zen is a prime example. In the Heian period (794–1186), leading priests of Kyoto went on perilous trips to China to study at the feet of the great masters, the result being the introduction of new types of Buddhist thought. In 1202, a temple was set up in Kyoto which challenged the established order, for it preached that the sole means of salvation was through Zen meditation. The name of the temple was Kennin-ji, and though it remained nominally part of the Tendai sect, it proved a pioneer for the new teaching.

Zen soon found favor with the ruling classes, first with the warrior regime in Kamakura and then with the imperial court in Kyoto. By the Muromachi period (1333–1573), when the Ashikaga shoguns made Kyoto their capital, Zen's place was assured and the whole arts and crafts of the age were affected as a result. A city

Zen temples have attractive wooden verandas which give onto gardens and provide a sense of oneness with nature, as here at Ikkyu-ji. In this way, the architecture fosters awareness of transience and the passing seasons.

The huge Sanmon gates of Zen temples are ceremonial in nature and feature altar rooms on the upper floor. Nanzen-ji is a noted example, the formidable size indicative of the temple's elevated status.

once known for aristocratic indulgence embraced a new order that spoke to essentialism and the suppression of self. Just 200 years after Myoan Eisai (1141–1215) had single-handedly introduced Zen to the city, seven mighty monasteries encircled the imperial capital. Robed figures with shaved heads roamed the corridors of power, while inside the thick temple walls, guarded by sturdy gates, monks rose before daybreak to begin a daily round of chanting, meditation and pondering anecdotes about eccentric Chinese masters.

Thanks to patronage from on high, the temples were able to acquire some exquisite decoration for their monks' quarters. Because of a desire to strip away illusion, the artwork had a minimalist character which tended towards simplicity and tranquility. Gardens were laid out by the top designers of the age, gorgeous *fusuma* paintings were executed by leading artists, and magnificent statues were commissioned for the halls of worship, while on the ceiling of the lecture halls were painted astonishing pictures of swirling dragons.

Following the Meiji Restoration of 1868, Buddhist temples in Japan have had to be self-financing. Income from visitors plays a vital role, and because of the attractiveness of Kyoto there can be formidable crowds of tourists at peak times. Some temples have embraced the opportunities this presents, while others are reluctant to compromise their religious purpose. Visitors looking for a moment of reflection during the periods of cherry blossom and maple viewing would be well advised to seek out a peaceful nook in one of the less famous temples. Those who are in earnest will rise at dawn to join the early morning *zazen* (sitting meditation) groups that welcome newcomers.

Sixty years ago, when temples were less frequented by tourists, Ruth Fuller Sasaki came to live at Daitoku-ji where she wrote of Kyoto in letters to the First Zen Institute of America. She had words of advice for her fellow country-men, and though much has changed in the meantime her words remain apposite.

I assume those who come to Japan for only a few weeks and hope to find out something about Zen in that time will come to Kyoto, for only in the old capital can at least the outer expressions of Zen still be found in abundance. Here are seven of the great Rinzai Zen headquarter

10

temples, each with its monastery. Here are the finest examples of Zen gardening. Here the old arts of Japan—Noh, tea ceremony, flower arrangement, *sumi* painting, calligraphy, pottery, among others—can best be enjoyed or studied…. There are a few rules you should lay down for yourself. The first is to put your camera away. Secondly, do not plan to do more than one major thing in one day. Thirdly, take your time and go leisurely…. When you return home and your friends ask you what you have learned about Zen in your three or four weeks' stay in Kyoto, probably you will have to say "Not much." Not much you can speak about, perhaps, but much you will never forget.

Since Fuller Sasaki's time, Zen has spread around the world, and today there are hundreds of training centers outside of Japan. None, of course, have the patina of age or the cultural wealth accumulated by the temples of Kyoto. This was highlighted in an exhibition put on in 2016 at the Kyoto National Museum to celebrate the 1,150th anniversary of the death, in 866, of Rinzai (the Chan Chinese Linji Yixuan), who introduced the oldest school of Zen to Japan. Paintings, statues, calligraphy and ritual items spoke of a keen aesthetic sense shaped by the indigenous taste for naturalness and purity.

Here in Kyoto's river basin, shielded by its protective hills, the Japanese sensibility has been nourished over long centuries. When the pursuit of beauty came into contact with the thinking of Zen, the result was an infusion of profundity and paradox, which gave rise to a remarkable aesthetic of minimalism. It is manifest in the awe-inspiring architecture, in gardens conducive to contemplation, in art that speaks of transcendence, and in calligraphy that is an art in itself. It marks one of mankind's greatest accomplishments, and it is one that deserves wider celebration. How better than through the discerning eye of John Einarsen, long-time devotee of the city and inspiration behind the award-winning *Kyoto Journal*? In the lens of his camera is captured a very special cultural heritage—the spirit of Zen. The spirit of Kyoto Zen.

The lotus blossom is a symbol of enlightenment for the way its pure beauty emerges from muddy depths. The flowers bloom from mid-June to early August and are seen to best effect in the Lotus Pond at Tenryu-ji.

Carp are a symbol of perseverance because of their determination to swim upstream. By achieving their aim, they became associated with such positive attributes as courage, strength and good fortune.

Water basins signify the importance of spiritual as well as physical purification. They are typically found beside pathways leading to tea houses, where the sound of flowing water serves to soothe the minds of visitors.

From China to Kyoto:
The Story of Zen Buddhism

Zen first emerged as a Buddhist sect in China, where it was known as Chan (meaning 'meditation'). Indeed, Zen is said to have originated in the encounter between Indian Buddhism and Chinese Daoism. Like other Buddhist sects, it refers back to the life and teaching of the historical Buddha, whose actual name was Siddharta Gautama. Since he was a prince of the Shaka clan, in Japan he is known as Shakyamuni ('sage of the Shaka') or Shaka Nyorai (Nyorai being a term for the Enlightened). After long years of ascetic practice, he was meditating under a bodhi tree when he experienced a deep realization that all people have Buddha nature and are endowed with wisdom and virtue but that they fail to realize this through being deluded.

For the rest of his life, Shakyamuni taught a message of salvation through spiritual awakening. His doctrine was based on the Four Noble Truths: life is suffering; suffering derives from desire fueled by the ego; there is need to overcome the ego; the way to do so is through the Noble Eightfold Path. Different sects emphasize different aspects of the teaching, and for Zen 'the flower sermon' holds particular significance. When Shakyamuni held up a single flower in silence, only one of his disciples smiled with understanding. He was named Mahakashyapa and Shakyamuni picked him as his 'Dharma heir' (successor in teaching). The incident encapsulates the essence of 'the wordless way', namely that truth is intuitive. As the Greek author Lafcadio Hearn (1850–1904) put it: "Zen represents human effort to reach through meditation zones of thought beyond the range of verbal expression."

As time passed, Buddhism spread across Asia and there developed a distinctive Southern and Northern Tradition, which differed over how best to strive for enlightenment. It was from the Northern Tradition, emphasizing compassion

One of Zen's most famous stories concerns a monk called Dazu Huike, who wanted to be a disciple of Bodhidharma. The legendary Zen founder showed little interest, however, famously sitting for years in front of a cave wall at Shaolin, so after repeated rejections Huike cut off his arm to prove his sincerity. The painting of *Huike Offering His Arm to Bodhidharma* was done by Sesshu Toyo in 1496.

for others, that emerged a legendary figure called Bodhi-dharma (Daruma in Japan). According to tradition, he was the 28th Patriarch, by which time Buddhism had become largely a matter of scholarship and good works. He is said to have sailed from India into China around 520, where he promoted the practice of meditation. Instead of seeking the truth in words and texts, he advocated looking within, as can be seen in a famous definition of Zen attributed to him:

> A special transmission outside the scriptures;
> Without dependence on words and symbols;
> Directly pointing at the heart of man;
> Seeing into one's nature and the attaining of
>   Buddhahood.

The emphasis on experiential knowledge is a vital element of Zen, and Shakyamuni's appointment of Mahakashyapa was the first in a teacher-disciple transmission of wisdom that has continued to the present day. In each case, the enlightenment of a disciple has to be verified by a master, and the lineage of such masters is a matter of importance in Zen.

Bodhidharma, or Daruma, remains a living presence in Zen temples, where pictures of him are often displayed. Many of these show him meditating in a cave, for tradition holds that he sat for nine years facing a cave wall in the mountains at Shaolin. Such was his determination not to fall asleep that he plucked out his own eyelids, as a result of which he is depicted with fierce features and bulging eyes. It is also said that he meditated so long that his legs and arms dropped off, which explains why Daruma dolls in Japan are shaped like a ball.

Transmission to Japan

As Chan Buddhism took hold in China, it was much influenced by Daoism, absorbing some of its thinking along with symbols and deities. Several favorite Zen anecdotes concern Daoist sages, and the often quoted "He who speaks does not know; he who knows does not speak" derives from Lao Tzu. By the ninth century, different Schools of Chan had appeared, amongst which was that of Linji

Yixuan, known in Japan as Rinzai (d. 866). His school was characterized by the severity of its practices, which were rooted in *zazen* (sitting meditation) and the study of *koan* (Zen riddles). At its heart was a belief that the rational self was an illusion and not the final arbiter of truth.

Meanwhile, in Japan a meditation hall had been established in Nara as early as the seventh century, and later a form of zazen was introduced to the monks on Mt Hiei. However, these early transmissions did not develop into a separate teaching, and it is only with Myoan Eisai (1141–1215) that Zen is considered to have taken hold in Japan. At the time, religion in the imperial capital was dominated by the eclectic Tendai and the esoteric Shingon sects. With the onset of *mappo* in Japanese Buddhism in the eleventh century, thought to be a time of degeneracy in Buddhist practice, many people had turned to belief in salvation through Amida, who vowed to receive in his Pure Land all those who called on him.

The arrival of Zen in the early 1200s coincided with the coming to power of the samurai. A military government had been set up at Kamakura in 1187, which proved fortuitous for the new sect, as warriors and monks shared similar values—austerity, endurance, subjugation of self, fearlessness in the face of death. (Buddhists, however, both clerics and the laity, took a pledge not to kill.) The *shogunate* saw a political advantage in promoting Zen as a means of weakening other sects (Tendai, in particular, had an independent army of warrior-monks). The Hojo clan, the power behind the *shogun*, saw in the new Zen culture an alternative to that of the aristocracy. With the adoption of Zen in this way, it seemed that the Buddhist sects had all carved out a niche for themselves: "Tendai for the emperor, Shingon for the aristocracy, Zen for warriors, and the Pure Land sect for the masses," was a popular saying.

The first temple to practice Zen in Kyoto was Kennin-ji, in 1202, but because of fierce pressure by the monks of Mt Hiei the monastery was forced to remain nominally part of Tendai. (It was only under the sixth abbot that it became fully Zen.) One of the early disciples at Kennin-ji, Eihei Dogen (1200–53), who had studied in China with a master from the Caodong School (J. Soto Zen), broke away to set up a temple in the south of Kyoto. The Tendai sect again acted to suppress a rival, prompting Dogen to leave the capital altogether after being offered land in what is present-day Fukui Prefecture, where in 1243 he founded Eihei-ji. It helps explain why Rinzai came to dominate Kyoto while Soto looked elsewhere.

The Gozan System

Major temples in China were often named after the mountain on which they were situated. In this way, 'mountain' came to be used as another word for temple. The Gozan system, literally 'Five Mountains,' referred to the official patronage of five major temples, and the Chinese model was taken up by the shogunate in Kamakura. In

Detail of one of the huge columns that support the Sanmon gate at Nanzen-ji. Hewn out of a zelkova in 1628, the column shows evidence of the passage of centuries.

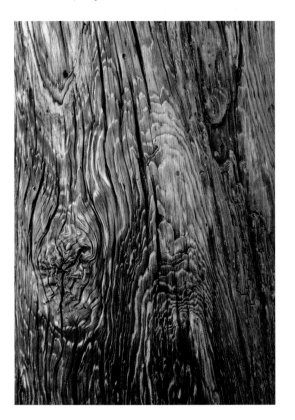

return for the donation of estates, the regime gained important rights, such as the power to appoint abbots, supervise standards and monitor financial affairs. The benefits to the temple thus came with a loss of independence.

The system started with five Kamakura temples (all Rinzai), and was then extended to Kyoto. In its final form, which was never rescinded, it consisted of five Kamakura temples and five Kyoto temples, with Nanzen-ji given supreme status above the two groupings. The Kyoto five comprised Tenryu-ji, Shokoku-ji, Kennin-ji, Tofuku-ji, and Manju-ji (now a subtemple of Tofuku-ji). Two notable exclusions were Daitoku-ji, which asked to be exempted to retain its independence, and Myoshin-ji, which chose to prioritize the practice of meditation.

In the Muromachi period (1333–1573), known as 'the Golden Age of Zen', the Ashikaga shoguns made Kyoto their capital and were powerful patrons of the Gozan temples. As a result, they became important centers of imported items and ideas, such as Neo-Confucianism. It inspired a period of creative vigor, exemplified by the Chinese ink paintings with their use of empty space. Gozan literature flourished, too, with an outpouring of poetry, treatises, diaries, commentaries and biographies, all written in Chinese. The new way of thinking—directly pointing at the heart of things—affected a range of art forms, from calligraphy and garden design to the tea ceremony, flower arrangement and Noh (whose creative genius, Zeami, was influenced by Soto Zen).

The arts of peacetime were halted by the destructiveness of the Onin War (1467–77), which devastated Kyoto and has been called one of the most futile wars ever fought. It started as a battle of succession to Ashikaga Yoshimitsu, founder of the Silver Pavilion, but with the passage of time the original cause was forgotten as rival armies stampeded across Kyoto. Fire raged throughout the city, and the mighty Zen complexes suffered along with everything else. As a result, most of the structures visible today date from rebuilding in the sixteenth century or later.

The civil war heralded a breakdown of central power, as Japan entered a period of Warring States when regional warlords vied with each other for power. Without the backing of a powerful shogun, the Gozan system fell into disarray, though ironically Zen as a whole prospered in the misfortune. The independent temples of Daitoku-ji and

The poet Hanshan and his friend Shide were a pair of eccentrics who lived near China's Mt Tiantai. Known in Japan as Kanzan and Jittoku, they became a popular subject in Zen painting. Kanzan lived in a cave and is depicted with a scroll to indicate his poetry, while Jittoku was a foundling who worked in the temple kitchen and passed food to his friend.

Myoshin-ji were boosted by donations from regional warlords for the establishment of subtemples. At the same time provincial rulers set up branch temples in their capitals. The top generals of the age received on the spot guidance from powerful Zen priests, who acted as negotiators or gave training in martial arts. Takuan Soho, briefly abbot of Daitoku-ji, is a famous example, drawing on Zen techniques to give much valued advice about swordsmanship.

The Edo Period and Modernization

With a return to stability under the Tokugawa shoguns, the country entered more settled times in the Edo Era (1600–1868). To counter the threat of Christianity, every family in the country was obliged to register with a Buddhist temple, and the *terakoya* system was introduced to promote public education by temple priests. With its Chinese roots Zen was well suited to promote the prevailing Neo-Confucianism. The connection was reinforced in 1654 by the arrival of a Chinese immigrant known in Japan as Ingen Ryuki (1592–1673), who not only introduced Obaku Zen but prompted an invigorating influx of Ming arts and crafts.

For Rinzai, the major development of these years was the work of Hakuin Ekaku (1686–1768), seen in hindsight as almost single-handedly reviving the moribund sect. He lived in a modest temple near the foot of Mt Fuji, turning down offers from Kyoto temples and devoting himself to the training of monks. He made a point of preaching to commoners and his drawing skills won him wide attention, particularly the idiosyncratic portraits of Daruma which he freely gave away. Such was his influence that it is said all contemporary Rinzai priests can trace their lineage back to him.

Following the Meiji Restoration of 1868, the new government was eager to establish a state religion as in the West. They chose the indigenous religion of Shinto and imposed its separation from Buddhism, to which it had been conjoined for over a thousand years. As a pillar of the discredited Tokugawa, Buddhism found itself in disfavor and its funding was cut. With the loss of their estates, temples became financially insolvent and had to sell off valuable assets, including parts of their precincts. As a result, some of Kyoto's Zen temples are barely a third or a quarter of their former size. Tenryu-ji is just one-tenth.

Buddhism was too deeply rooted to be eradicated, however, and it soon made a comeback. Priests became dependent to a large extent on funeral rites for their income. For many Japanese, the only encounter with Buddhism is through the death of a family member, when the elaborate obsequies involved in securing a safe passage into the afterworld can cost millions of yen. However, this too has come under threat in recent years as Japan's population shrinks, particularly in rural areas. It is said that in the next couple of decades as many as a third of Japan's 77,000 Buddhist temples are expected to close down.

To some extent, Zen in Kyoto has been shielded against the downward trend because of the tourist trade, which has seen a dramatic rise in numbers. Kyoto, a city of a million and a half, now attracts over 50 million visitors a year. For a religious sect that values silent contemplation, the revenue from tourists is a mixed blessing, as indicated by this notice posted publicly at Shokoku-ji: "Please respect the temple precincts, garden and environment as a religious space and keep all noise to a minimum. You will acquire Buddha's providence from the bottom of our heart."

Zen Spreads to the West

During the course of the twentieth century, as knowledge of Zen spread to the West, Kyoto played a prominent part. D. T. Suzuki (1870–1966) is a case in point. Born in Kanazawa, Suzuki studied Zen in Kamakura before working for eleven years in America. After returning to Japan and teaching English in Tokyo, he took up a professorship at Kyoto's Otani University in 1921, where he continued teaching until the age of 89. He founded the influential Eastern Buddhist Society, and in 1927 published the first series of his ground-breaking *Essays in Buddhism*. Other books followed, among them *An Introduction to Zen Buddhism* in 1934 and *Zen and Japanese Culture* in 1959. Over the years, Suzuki gave several lecture tours in the West, described as more like Buddhist sermons than academic talks. Although he has been hailed for his pioneering work, he has also proved a controversial figure who has come under criticism for espousing essentialism.

Among Western intellectuals to take an early interest in Zen were such notables as Satre, Heisenberg, Huxley, Jung and Heidegger. The Beat Generation of the 1950s looked East for inspiration, with Kerouac dubbing his book *Dharma Bums* (1958) and Gary Snyder coming to Kyoto to study Zen. (Other poets to have found inspiration in Kyoto include Kenneth Rexroth, Cid Corman and Edith Shiffert.) But perhaps the most influential figure of all was Ruth Fuller Sasaki (1892–1967), whose pioneering work played a vital role in opening up Zen to the West.

As Ruth Fuller, she had met Suzuki in 1930 while on a trip to Japan, and she returned to Kyoto the following year to do zazen meditation at a Nanzen-ji subtemple. As a wealthy widow following the death of her husband, she had continued her Zen practice in America, marrying the Japanese master Sokei Sasaki shortly before his death. In accordance with his wishes, she set up the First Zen Institute of America and traveled on its behalf to Kyoto in 1949. She was given use of a house in Daitoku-ji, and used her wealth to develop the site into the subtemple of Ryosen-an. Here she entertained such luminaries as Joseph Campbell, R. H. Blyth and her son-in-law Alan Watts. She was a formidable woman, at one time sitting zazen eighteen hours a day, and she dedicated herself to making Zen

writings available to the English-speaking world. To that end, she created a research team, which included Gary Snyder, Burton Watson and Philip Yampolsky.

During the 1960s and 1970s, Zen experienced a cultish boom in the West fueled by books as disparate as *The Way of Zen* (1957) and *Zen and the Art of Motorcycle Maintenance* (1974). The spiritually displaced headed for 'a golden triangle' of Kathmandu, Kuta and Kyoto, and the streets of the city began to fill with seekers of *satori* ('awakening'). Some returned home none the wiser, though others stayed on in the city to pursue their interest long term. Some even qualified as priests. Figures like 'Shakuhachi Bob' were prominent among the foreign community, and the appeal of studying Zen in the city was poetically caught by Pico Iyer in *The Lady and the Monk* (1991).

The diffusion to the West has been compared by commentators to the movement of Zen from China to Japan. Among the Kyoto priests facilitating the westward spread were Zenkei Shibayama at Nanzen-ji, a follower of D. T. Suzuki; the abbot of Tofuku-ji, Keido Fukushima, who was unusually open to teaching Western students; and Soko Morinaga, head of Hanazono University, who was the inspiration behind Daishu-in West in northern California and the Zen Centre in London. Through the work of such figures, Kyoto's reputation as a citadel of Zen has been spread around the world. Eight hundred years after its establishment in the city, a religion based on sitting has proved remarkably mobile.

Incense serves as a purifying agent in Buddhism and is offered at times of worship. Since an incense stick burns on average for 30–40 minutes, it is used in Zen to measure the length of meditation sessions.

WAYS TO STILLNESS:
THE THREE SECTS OF ZEN

Contrary to the perceptions of many in the West, Zen is not the dominant strand of Buddhism in Japan. In terms of followers, the Pure Land and Nichiren faiths (if one includes the lay organization Soka Gakkai) are bigger, as is the esoteric Shingon sect. Moreover, within Zen there are three different schools: Rinzai, Soto and Obaku. Rinzai is the oldest, Soto the biggest, Obaku the smallest.

Of the 20,000 Zen temples in Japan, Soto has about 75 percent, yet in Kyoto it is Rinzai that is dominant. Indeed, of the 35 temples and subtemples included in this book, only three are Soto (Kosho-ji, Shisendo and Genko-an) while just two are Obaku (Manpuku-ji and Kanga-an). How is this explained? An old saying suggests the answer: "Rinzai for warriors, Soto for commoners." While Rinzai appealed to the élite of Kyoto, Soto spread in the provinces with the support of regional lords. (Obaku was a latecomer.)

Of the three Zen sects, Rinzai and Obaku are the closest in thinking, for both trace their lineage back to the Chinese master Linji Yixuan (d. 866; Rinzai in Japanese). The difference can best be understood in terms of history. Rinzai arrived from Song China in the late twelfth century and subsequently became Japanized. Obaku arrived from Ming China in the mid-seventeenth century and retained many of its Chinese forms and regulations. The doctrinal differences are slight, however, and in recent times they have joined together in an association in which Obaku stands alongside Rinzai's fourteen schools (which are mainly a matter of lineage).

The difference between Rinzai and Soto is more substantial. Rinzai sees meditation as a means to awakening, whereas Soto sees it as an end in itself. "Practice and enlightenment are one," said Eihei Dogen, founder of the sect. For Soto, just sitting (*shikantaza*) is in itself transformative, and the striving of Rinzai is seen as counterproductive. In its attempt to trigger awakening, Rinzai makes more use of *koan* than Soto, which looks rather to

Monks at Shokoku-ji emerge from the monastery's kitchen, known as *kuri*. Over time, the quarters evolved to house temple offices and to function as an administrative center. The bell-shaped windows and doors that open outwards were features introduced from China.

intensity of meditation. Rinzai is known as the rough school, using a sudden sharp shock to jolt the sitter into enlightenment. Soto is known as the gentle school, taking a gradual approach.

In terms of the master–pupil relationship, the Rinzai master is said to be like a wise general ably directing his students, while the Soto master resembles a wise farmer, concerned with nourishing his plants. The difference in approach goes along with differences in practice: Rinzai does *zazen* facing the center of the room, Soto faces towards the wall. There is a distinction also in the length and manner of holding the *kyousaku*, the stick used for hitting sitters. As for walking meditation (*kinhin*), Rinzai prefers a brisk energetic manner with left hand wrapped round right wrist; Soto adopts a slow pace, with right hand wrapped round left. Such distinctions are of little significance, however, compared with the difference in emphasis, for while both aim at attaining a state of compassion, Rinzai is inclined to shout "Wake up!" whereas Soto urges "Just sit!"

Eat, Sit, Sleep:
The Daily Routine of a Zen Monk

The seven great Zen temples of Kyoto each head a separate school of Rinzai Zen. These schools are administratively distinct but basically the same with regard to practice and teachings, and Zen priests are free to move from one school to another. Each school is headed by a chief abbot who is a qualified Zen master or venerable teacher (*roshi*). Assisting him in his duties are senior prelates, almost all of whom serve as priests at their own temples. Rinzai was originally a celibate tradition, but following the end of Japanese feudalism in 1868 the government authorized marriage for Buddhist monks as part of a program to weaken the

A thick wooden block is struck like a gong to summon monks for functions. This one from Manpuku-ji has a Chinese inscription that reads "All who practice the way, pay attention! Birth and death are grave matters. Nothing is permanent; time passes quickly. Awake! Do not dawdle; devote yourself to your practice."

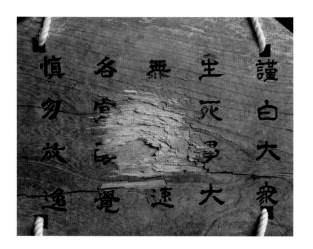

religion. Although most of Kyoto's great monastic abbots maintain the custom of celibacy, it is no longer obligatory.

To enter the Zen clergy it is first necessary to become the disciple of a temple priest. In the majority of cases, this means the son of a priest registering as a disciple of his father (Japan maintains the hereditary principle in several areas of traditional life). Laypeople are able to become disciples of a local priest or a priest with whom they practiced *zazen* sitting mediation. They will typically spend a year or two at the priest's temple, then have an ordination ceremony qualifying them to enter a training monastery.

Entrance to the training monastery (known in Rinzai as *sodo* or *senmon dojo*) involves arriving at the entrance hall early in the morning and presenting the necessary documents from the ordaining priest. Applicants are refused entry for two days as a test of resolve. After waiting patiently for the two days, they are moved from the entrance hall to a small room where they must meditate for five days facing the wall. Only when this trial period is completed are they accepted into the monastic community.

Zen Training

The Zen sodo is basically a training hall. It is not, as in Christianity, a cloister in which to spend one's life. Monks who wish to become temple priests are asked to train for at least three years. In this case, the sodo serves the function of a seminary. However, monks who are interested in a life of meditation remain at the monastery many years longer in order to advance as far as they can, which involves working on and passing *koan* (Zen riddles). In this case, they stay until they have completed the training process, something that can take from twelve to twenty years.

The few monks who finish the entire koan curriculum and are judged to have the qualities necessary to teach others receive a certificate of approval known as *inka shomei*, which qualifies them to become a Zen roshi. For such individuals it is common to undergo a period of post-monastic training, lasting several years, before they assume their teaching duties.

Just a few decades ago, Rinzai monasteries comprised communities of thirty or more monks, but nowadays, with the steep decline in the number of young people in Japan, most *sodo* manage with ten monks or fewer. The training consists of zazen, koan study, sutra chanting, physical labor (known as *samu*) and *takuhatsu* (begging for alms in nearby communities). However, zazen is central, for the meditative mind should be maintained even during all the other activities.

The formal practice of zazen occupies up to seven hours a day of the normal schedule. It is the basic technique by which practitioners seek to awaken to levels of mind deeper than discursive thought. By observing the mind's workings, the practitioner comes to realize the illusory nature of the ego, which is basically no more than a construct of thought. This leads to a deeper understanding of the mind as something that is empty yet dynamic in nature. Ironically, in losing the sense of self, the meditator finds oneness with everything. Realization of this is called *kensho* ('seeing one's original nature').

Koan are enigmatic problems that cannot be solved with the rational mind, such as, "What was your original face before you were born?" or "Does a dog have Buddha nature?" If used properly, they allow the practitioner to access a new mode of understanding beyond logical thought. In monastic practice, koan are assigned to students and their progress checked by the roshi during interviews. Once the master is satisfied with a student's understanding, he assigns a different koan to deepen and refine the newly acquired insight. Traditionally, there are said to be 1,700 koan in all, though the number employed by any particular master varies considerably.

There are two main styles of *zazen* sitting meditation. That of the Rinzai and Obaku sects is done facing inwards towards the center of the room, whereas the Soto style is done facing the wall.

The Daily Routine

Apart from the formal practice of zazen, much of the monastic day is taken up with physical work, which is considered a vital means of cultivating mindfulness and distinguishes the Zen monastery from other Buddhist sects. Indeed, a Zen saying states that cleaning comes first, then religious practice, and thirdly study. By focusing on the job in hand, monks free the mind of needless distraction. Tasks include sweeping the grounds, cleaning, splitting firewood, cultivating vegetables and preparing food. As one wag put it, for people who sit around all day, there is a lot of hard work involved.

The monk's life is carefully regulated, and first-timers are often startled by the military-style promptitude with which activities are carried out. This contrasts with the romantic image prevalent in the West. As Pico Iyer puts it in *The Lady and the Monk* (1991): "The Zen life is like a mountain wrapped in mist—though it looks beautiful from afar, once you start climbing there's nothing but hard rock."

The daily schedule differs between monasteries and there are variations according to season, but the basic routine is essentially the same. Early rising is followed by sutra chanting, zazen, cleaning and physical chores. Meals are carried out in silence. Takuhatsu mendicancy is conducted at least twelve mornings a month, while bathing is reserved

Takuhatsu is the practice of begging for alms, whereby young monks in single file are led through neighborhoods intoning "Hooo ... hooo...." (meaning Dharma). Donating food and money is rewarded with sutra chanting, which brings spiritual merit. Here a young monk in outfit holds out his satchel-bag for offerings, bearing the words Tenryu Sodo (Tenryu monks' quarters).

for days with a four or nine in them (i.e. every five days). A typical day may run as follows, though it is not prescribed:

4 am Wake up

4.10–5 am Sutra chanting

5–7 am Zazen and interview with abbot

7 am Breakfast of rice gruel, salted plum and pickles

8–10.50 am Cleaning and work duties

11 am Lunch, typically barley rice, miso soup, cooked vegetable and pickled radish

1–3.50 pm Work duty

4 pm Light meal similar to lunch

5–8.30 pm Zazen and interview with abbot

9 pm Lights out

9–11 pm Night sitting

The monthly one-week intensive retreats called *sesshin* involve a greater focus on zazen and koan study. There may be twelve to fourteen hours of meditation (including night sitting) and up to four koan interviews a day. At a number of monasteries, laypeople are allowed to participate, living in the training hall where they are allotted a single tatami mat and a futon for sleeping. "Half a mat when awake [for zazen]; a whole mat when asleep" runs a Zen saying. For the duration of the sesshin, this small area represents the entire universe, channeling practitioners to look within. For some, the result may be a deep awakening.

THROUGH FOREIGN EYES:
AN INTERVIEW WITH THOMAS YUHO KIRCHNER

Thomas Kirchner is a Rinzai monk and caretaker of Rinsen-ji, a temple which is part of the Tenryu-ji complex in Arashiyama. Born in Baltimore in 1949, Kirchner came to Japan in 1969 for a one-year course at Waseda University, following which he stayed on to pursue an interest in Zen. In 1974 he was ordained as a monk and given the name Shaku Yuho, spending time at Kencho-ji in Kamakura and later at Kennin-ji in Kyoto. He holds a master's degree from Otani University (where D. T. Suzuki taught) and is a researcher at Hanazono University, the Rinzai Zen university. Amongst his publications are *Entangling Vines*, a collection of 272 *koan*; *Dialogues in a Dream*, a translation and biography of Muso Soseki; and an annotated translation of *The Record of Linji*, completing work left behind by Ruth Fuller Sasaki.

How did you first become interested in Zen?
As a young boy growing up in the 1960s, I read the books around at that time—D. T. Suzuki, Alan Watts, Philip Kapleau. Also Eugen Herrigel, whose book on archery led me to take it up in Japan. But it wasn't just books, because during my first year at college I was deeply moved by Zenkei Shibayama, abbot of Nanzen-ji, whose talk I attended. He must have been in his seventies, but his bright, peaceful eyes and cheerful personality moved me deeply. Unlike some other Eastern sages I'd met, he didn't seem to be selling anything.

What was the first practical step you took in pursuing Zen?
After studying at Waseda, I stayed on and wanted to try meditation. My archery teacher recommended a temple in Tokyo, which led me to want to explore Zen more fully. Through a contact there, I was introduced to a small temple in Nagano where there were only four people: the *roshi*, his wife, another practitioner and myself. Later I spent a few years as a lay monk at the monastery

Shofuku-ji in Kobe. In 1974, after I was ordained as a monk, I spent four years at Kencho-ji in Kamakura and three years at Kennin-ji in Kyoto.

Monastic life is known for its hardships, so i wonder how you coped with that?
It's something you get used to. The early mornings, the painful sitting, the cold in winter. It's not easy at first as you have to retrain all your bad habits. But after a few years correct posture becomes natural and the pain recedes.

For a while you looked outside monastic life. As well as a master's degree, you did an MEd, trained in acupuncture and *shiatsu*, and took a job as copyeditor at Nanzan University.
Yes, my parents wanted me to graduate (I had dropped out of college in America), so I came to Kyoto to study while teaching English and living in a tea house in Daitoku-ji. I wanted to see if there was something more to life.

But you went back to monastic life?
The reason was in the late 1990s I developed a tumor in my pancreas. My weight dropped from 70 kilos to below 50, and I was expected to die. But when it came to the operation and they cut me open, there was nothing but healthy tissue. The tumor had mysteriously disappeared. It was a life-changing event; as the old saying goes, "The proximity of death wonderfully clarifies the mind." While thinking over my life, I found the most meaningful part was the time I spent in monasteries. Everything else seemed superficial, pleasant to be sure, but inconsequential.

How did you get such a prestigious position as looking after the temple where the famed Zen master Muso Soseki lived and is buried?
It was through people who knew me from my earlier spells in monasteries. If you live with people in a monastery for any length of time, you get to know them very well, like army buddies. It's very intimate, and there's a level of trust that you build up. So people who knew me asked if I would be interested in looking after the property (it had been empty for two years).

What do you have to do?
I maintain the grounds and rake the garden, which I think is the largest dry landscape in Kyoto, maybe even in the whole country.

It takes a couple of hours a week. I also show visitors around, and I help out if there are foreigners on short courses at the monastery. It's a life that suits me, as I enjoy physical work like growing organic vegetables and wheat.

What's your impression of Zen in Kyoto?
Kyoto is the heart of Zen culture, so not surprisingly it tends to be conservative. There are centuries of tradition to maintain. Some people talk of a decline, but part of that is simply the falling population. Numbers are down in all walks of life. But there's another factor, I think. Five hundred years ago there was a vitality about Zen because the level of suffering and the awareness of death was much more intense. Modern medicine shields us from that, and there's so much distraction in modern life, such as the media and electronics. Religion is so far removed from daily life that some young people don't even know what Zen is. But having said that, there's a great spiritual thirst which materialism can't satisfy. And there are still some truly inspiring *roshi* around. That gives me great hope for the future.

Whereas straw sandals are worn for *takuhatsu* alms begging (see opposite), wooden sandals known as *geta* are worn around the temple or on outings. These have white straps instead of the usual black in order to distinguish monks from laypersons.

Finding One's Way:
The Design of a Zen Monastery

Kyoto has seven great Zen temple-monasteries, which dominate the city's landscape. In order of foundation, these are Kennin-ji (1202), Tofuku-ji (1236), Nanzen-ji (1291), Daitoku-ji (1326), Tenryu-ji (1339), Myoshin-ji (1342) and Shokoku-ji (1382). Their design differs from the temples of earlier Buddhism and their architecture was a borrowing from Song China (960–1279). The layout correlates with that of the human body, so that the Buddha Hall lies at its heart and a straight spine runs through the main buildings. As in the Chinese tradition, the compound was aligned towards the south and comprises a set of seven structures. Apart from the Buddha Hall, there is a Sanmon (ceremonial gate); a Doctrine or Lecture Hall; a Meditation Hall; and a kitchen, latrine and bath. The name of each is displayed prominently on a wooden plaque below the eaves.

The main structures are Chinese in character, with buildings set directly on the ground and floors made of stone or tile. The woodwork is unpainted and the large wooden doors swing open rather than slide, Japanese-style. Zen is characterized by rigid and structured practice, and thus the cavernous halls give off an air of austerity in keeping with the life of the monks. The walkways between buildings are wide, suited to large processions, and though they may be decorated with trees, there are no ornamental gardens and the atmosphere is spartan.

Around this central Chinese core are subtemples in Japanese style, with tatami, asymmetry and residential architecture. They have a more intimate feel. Shoes are taken off and tatami rooms are separated by narrow corridors open

to delightful gardens. These subtemples developed organically, by contrast with the symmetry and straight lines of the monastic buildings. The prime example is the Myoshin-ji complex, with 46 subtemples arranged like a medieval village centered around a church. The subtemples are privately owned, and although the head priest participates in monastic affairs, the building constitutes his family residence.

Some of the monasteries have lost their original layout or were conceived differently from the outset. Nanzen-ji, for instance, is aligned on an east–west axis, because it originated as a villa owned by a retired emperor. Others have been badly affected by disaster, particularly the Onin War (1467–77), which devastated the entire city. Indeed,

the large temples have without exception all burned to the ground at least once. Some structures were never replaced, and others have been rebuilt several times over the course of their history. But while wood can be a liability in terms of fire, it can also be an advantage in terms of relocation, and several temples have benefitted from the gift of imperial palace buildings or magnificent castle gates.

Nearly every temple displays a large painted illustration of the grounds. Although fairly recent, these boards originated in an earlier tradition of *keidaizu*, prints of the compound common in the Edo period (1600–1868). This painted guide to Shokoku-ji shows its subsidiary temples of Kinkaku-ji and Ginkaku-ji in the top left and bottom right, respectively.

TEMPLE STRUCTURES

To fully appreciate the temple compounds, it should be borne in mind that when constructed the huge monastic buildings would have dominated the cityscape. Magnificent views over the capital were afforded from the upper floor of the large ceremonial gates. Sadly, in an age of modern high-rises, the wooden buildings have lost some of their former grandeur although the dimensions and woodwork are still awe-inspiring.

❶ Outer Gate (Somon) This is the general entrance, situated slightly off the central axis. It generally faces south in accordance with Chinese fengshui principles, with important buildings towards the north of the complex.

❷ Imperial Messenger's Gate (Chokushimon) The ceremonial gate is reserved for the emperor and his envoys, signifying the importance of imperial patronage in the past. It stands on the monastery's central axis and is normally kept shut.

❸ Hanchi This pond at the entrance to Zen temples, often square in shape and with an arched stone bridge, represents passing from profane into sacred space. The lotus is a symbol of enlightenment because of its ability to produce a pure and beautiful flower from muddy depths. The ponds also served as a source of water during the conflagrations to which temples were prone.

❹ Sanmon (Ceremonial Gate) Sanmon means 'mountain gate' (the word mountain is synonymous with temple). It is symbolic rather than functional, typically with an altar room on its second floor. It is also known as Enlightenment Gate since it represents the passage into the world of Zen. In some cases, the first of the Chinese characters is written as 'three' instead of 'mountain' to denote the three openings in the gate that represent 'emptiness', 'no-mind' and 'no intention'. The space between the Sanmon and the next structure is planted with trees, which are used for rebuilding.

❺ Buddha Hall (Butsuden) Normally standing on the north–south axis between the Sanmon gate and the Lecture Hall, this houses the temple's main object of worship. The building was the second largest after the Dharma Hall and its high ceiling and stone floor are thought to have enhanced the chanting of sutra. Most Kyoto monasteries no longer have one because the originals were not replaced after being burnt down (it was also felt that too much ritual distracted from Zen practice). Both Daitoku-ji and Myoshin-ji still have Buddha Halls.

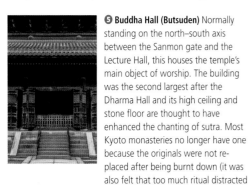

❻ Dharma Hall/Lecture Hall (Hatto or Hodo) This formidable temple building, with its gleaming tiled roof and sweeping eaves, houses statues of deities, guardian figures and statues of former abbots and is also used for formal talks by the abbot. The columns supporting the roofs are made of sturdy zelkova (*keyaki*) wood. The slightly curved 'mirror ceilings' bear magnificent paintings of dragons, thought to help guard against fire and evil spirits. Shielded beneath the dragons' protection, the Dharma could be preached without fear.

❼ Meditation Hall (Zendo or Sodo) This hall plays a vital role in the monastery. Along the sides runs a raised platform on which monks sit in *zazen* meditation on *zabuton* cushions. The open space in the middle may be used for walking meditation. There is usually an image of Monju, bodhisattva of wisdom, whose *vajra* sword cuts through all delusion. The meditation space is combined with a training hall, where monks are allotted one tatami on which to live, with storage for bedding and shelving for a few possessions.

⑫ Bell Tower (Shoro) The monastery's largest bell is rung at dawn and dusk each day. As at other temples, it is also struck 108 times for the New Year, each strike ringing out one of the attachments to which humans are prey.

⑬ Sutra Hall (Kyozo) A small building with shelving for storage of sutras and other documents. The sutras are scriptures passed down by tradition as the legacy of the historical Buddha. Originally, these were transmitted orally (in Pali) by his disciples, in particular Ananda. Different sects of Buddhism privilege certain sutra, and for Zen it is the Heart Sutra (Hannya Shingyo).

⑭ Founder's Hall (Kaisando) This is a hall for veneration of the founding figure of the monastery where special memorial services are held.

⑮ Subtemples (Tachu) Over the centuries, subtemples proliferated along the sides of the main temple axis. Many contain items of great value, such as paintings, dry landscape gardens and rustic tea houses. Most were funded by powerful patrons and staffed by monks who had retired from formal duties. Some were constructed by samurai who had converted to Zen and wanted to pursue a religious life.

⑪ Abbot's Quarters (Hojo) The Japanese name Hojo translates as 'Ten Foot Square Hut', indicative of how small the original area was. Over time, as Zen was patronized by those in power, the Abbot's Quarters became an important meeting place and grew in prestige. A covered walkway connected the building to the Lecture Hall (Hatto/Hodo), to which the abbot would proceed in his finery to deliver the important Dharma talk. *Fusama* sliding doors divided the area into six sections, with three south-facing rooms for entertaining dignitaries and three north-facing rooms for more private purposes. Generally speaking, the southern set contain a central altar flanked by sliding screens painted by famous artists, and the rooms look onto a courtyard covered with fine white gravel to provide a dignified air. The northern rooms typically have a living area, a study and a room for meeting acolytes. These look onto a more informal type of garden, sometimes used by the abbot for instructional purposes.

⑨ Latrine (Tousu) The traditional toilet comprises a circular hole in the earthen floor. To cater for large numbers, neat rows of such holes were housed in a long wooden building. (The restored latrines at Tofuku-ji, oldest and largest of its type, catered for a hundred people at a time.) In the past, human excrement was a major source of income for the temples as it was used for manure and delivered to the estates of nobles and samurai warriors.

⑧ Kitchen (Kuri) Traditionally, the kitchen is situated next to the Abbot's Quarters. Many monasteries have vegetable gardens to cater for the vegetarian diet of the monks, with a typical meal comprising rice, miso soup, a vegetable side dish, pickles and green tea.

⑩ Baths (Yokushitsu) The bath house used steam to conserve natural resources, since conventional baths would have consumed an inordinate amount of wood and water. There was a highly prescribed ritual for bathing, which was considered a form of spiritual practice. There are restored bath houses at Shokoku-ji, Myoshin-ji and Tofuku-ji. (In smaller institutions, the kitchen, latrine and baths were housed in a single building.)

⑯ Shinto Shrines (Jinja) The custom of paying respect to guardian deities (*kami*) was part of the Japanese tradition before the arrival of Zen, and continues today. In some cases, shrines were already in place before monasteries were built, and they were maintained for protective reasons. Other shrines were added later, even as recently as the late nineteenth century when Buddhism fell out of favor (and over 20,000 temples were destroyed). Temples sought to appease the authorities by establishing Shinto shrines to show compliance with the new state religion.

Visions of Serenity:
The Zen Garden

Bonsai originated in China and was adopted by the Japanese following the introduction of Zen. The tray here was a New Year's gift to Taizo-in and features the 'three friends of winter'—plum, pine and bamboo. Tending to temple gardens takes up to seven full days a month.

Japanese gardens have a long history, stretching back even before the pleasure gardens of Heian nobles (794–1186). These featured a pond around which were set villas and pavilions. Here aristocratic pursuits took place, such as fishing, moon-viewing, poetry writing and boating. Shorelines were replicated by rocks along the margin of a pond and waterfalls were reproduced by water emerging from between rocks. Some of the gardens were given a spiritual dimension by evocations of Amida's western paradise, with its promise of salvation. By the eleventh century, the sophisticated gardening knowledge had been collected in Japan's first book on the subject, *Sakuteiki* (Notes on Garden Construction).

Kyoto's flourishing garden culture was facilitated by the city's location in a river basin. In the forested surrounds were plentiful resources of wood and stone. Added to this was fresh-flowing water and underground springs. Moreover, the humid climate lends itself to the cultivation of moss, which grows easily on untended soil (Japan has only 0.25 percent of the Earth's surface but is home to nearly 10 percent of known moss varieties).

With the introduction of Zen, a new of type of thinking permeated garden design. Rather than a place to enter, the garden became a place to view. As a consequence, most of the gardens in Zen temples are enclosed, as if to frame the scene and stop the mind from wandering. It is worth noting,

Rocks can be appreciated in their own right as aesthetic objects, though they may also be invested with symbolic significance. In the dry garden at Ryogin-an, laid out by Mirei Shigemori in 1964, they represent a dragon emerging from the sea and about to fly up to heaven (the mythical creature has the attributes of both fish and bird).

Japanese gardens often feature a set of three rocks, such as that above sited on a rise at Komyo-in. The grouping represents a Buddhist triad, whereby an enlightened being is flanked by two attendants. In Zen this denotes the Shaka triad, in which the historical Buddha, known in Japan as Shakyamuni, is accompanied by two bodhisattva, Fugen and Monju.

however, that there is no such term as 'Zen garden' in Japanese. Rather, there are garden types that have been adapted to a Zen setting. Although they come in various forms, they share underlying characteristics to do with a lack of ostentation, an inclination to tranquility, a tendency for symbolism and an 'elegant mystery' (*yugen*). The Daoist connections are reflected in a sense of flow and the frequent reference to Chinese myth.

One of the earliest examples is the Sogenchi pond garden at Tenryu-ji. It was laid out by the founder, Muso Soseki (1275–1351), who in one of his writings warned against a worldly love of gardens. His intention was rather for the garden to serve a spiritual purpose, and the landscaped grounds draw in the surrounding hills to speak of oneness with nature. In this way, his creation is not simply an adornment but a lesson in Zen thinking.

The Dry Landscape

The type of garden most closely associated with Zen is the dry landscape (*karesansui*). At its most basic it simply consists of raked gravel or sand. The style originated in China, where it was found useful for areas lacking water, and it developed into a three-dimensional counterpart to Chinese ink painting. Its adoption in Kyoto stemmed from a number of factors, one of which was economic. With the collapse of the central government in the Warring States or Sengoku period in Japan (1467–1568), there were few powerful patrons to fund expensive gardens. The large pond gardens required a lot of land and labor. By contrast, the dry landscape only required a small area of pebbles and rocks. Moreover, maintenance was easy as a single monk could manage the raking and sweeping.

One of the most common features at Zen temples is the Horai garden, as here at Ryogen-in. Mythical Mt Horai constitutes one of a small group of islands where Daoist Immortals dwell, represented by the rock grouping in the corner. This is accompanied by two symbolic islands, that of the Turtle (in the circle of moss) and that of the Crane (vertical to signify the long neck). Together the creatures symbolize longevity and happiness.

The new style was particularly well suited to Kyoto because of the abundance of gravel brought into the city by rivers flowing down from the granite hillsides. It was favored by Zen because of its representational qualities. Raked gravel suggested open expanses of sea, or space, or eternity. The rocks spoke of moments in time, thoughts in the mind or islands in an ocean. The enigmatic nature of the compositions offered a visual counterpart to Zen riddles. "What is the meaning of the Buddha mind?" asks a well-known *koan*. "A single pine growing in a garden," runs the answer.

A common form of dry landscape is the Horai Garden (Penglai in English). This refers to the ancient Chinese belief in the Isles of the Immortals, where people live happily free of the ills that plague ordinary humans. Dominating the four Isles is mythical Mt Horai, which is represented by a rock grouping out of which flows 'the river of life'. In this ideal place is a symbolic meeting place of human and heavenly worlds, where opposites are brought together in harmonious coexistence, signifying the underlying oneness of things.

The unity of opposites is manifest in the form of Turtle and Crane Islands (the animals are Chinese emblems of longevity and good fortune). While the turtle can plunge to the depths, the crane can soar to the heights, so that in their coming together the world of division is symbolically transcended. Turtle and Crane Islands can be found in pond gardens as well as dry landscapes, with the crane represented by a vertical arrangement (as if about to take off) and the turtle by more horizontal features. In some cases, the islands are reduced to a simple yin–yang pairing of rocks, one vertical and one horizontal.

A TEA GARDEN

Another type of garden often found at Zen temples is that leading to a tea house. Rather than an object for viewing, the purpose here is to act as a passage between the mundane world of everyday life and the more serene world of the tea house. The Japanese term is *roji*, which means 'dewy path', and the materials are sober and subdued: moss, rocks, shrubs, bamboo, stone lantern and wash basin. They serve to calm the soul as the visitor prepares for the contemplative nature of the tea ceremony. "The garden serves the human soul," writes Preston Houser. "It is a secular stage whereupon our spirituality is brought into play."

The approach consists of a series of thresholds, and the effect is of entering deeper into nature. The route is determined by a path of stepping stones, set closely together for those wearing kimono. A sense of distance is conveyed by the winding course it follows, as if in keeping with the natural contours of the land. Near the tea house stands a water bowl for ablutions, symbolically purifying spirit as well as body. In this way, by removal of 'the dust of the world', the visitor enters into a different realm.

Kyoto boasts the finest collections of tea rooms in the world. Many are centuries old and made of fragile materials: bamboo, paper, earth. Some require special permission to enter or are only open to official groups. Several are off-limits to visitors altogether. Those that are available for inspection are often models of *wabi-sabi*, the aesthetic of rustic austerity. At the end of the garden path, it turns out, is a lesson in harmony with nature.

The tea garden is known in Japanese as *roji*, meaning 'dewy path' leading to the tea house. That of Koto-in provides a typical example, with a simple rustic gate separating the outer garden with its trees and bushes from the more sedate and sparse inner garden.

Sipping Zen:
The Japanese Tea Ceremony

Top and above The tea served at Zen temples is *matcha*, made by whisking hot water and green tea powder. This is served in a bowl of aesthetic or historic significance, with particular attention paid to the color contrast with the tea. The somewhat bitter taste is offset by the sweetness of the accompanying confectionery.

The tea ceremony as we know it today was initiated in Kyoto's monasteries, and it came to fruition in the sixteenth century under a series of tea masters trained in Zen. Even though aristocrats had indulged in tea ceremonies in earlier times, it was mostly for pleasure and display. But with the introduction of Zen, the suppression of self came together with the pursuit of beauty, the result being one of the world's great cultural practices. In this way the simple partaking of tea was imbued with a strong spiritual component, showcasing many of Japan's finest traits: refinement, exactitude, attention to detail and an unerring aesthetic sense. In all of this, Zen played such a vital role that a traditional saying states that "Zen and tea have the same taste."

It all began in 1191 when Myoan Eisai, founder of Kennin-ji, brought back tea seeds from China. Tea drinking had entered Japan in earlier times but had died out, and Eisai reintroduced the practice not only by passing on seeds for plantation but by promoting its life-enhancing qualities. He also advocated its use as an antidote to falling asleep during meditation. Accordingly, green tea became a feature of Zen life, with the preparation and consumption conducted according to Chinese practice. With the passage of time, the ritual was adapted to Japanese tastes, and amongst leading contributors were Zen priests such as Ikkyu Sojun and his disciple Murata Shuko, both with ties to Daitoku-ji (later dubbed 'the head temple of tea').

Murata Shuko was tea master to the aesthete-shogun Ashikaga Yoshimasa, for whom he built a four-and-a-half mat tea room at the Silver Pavilion. It became the prototype for later models. Shuko also introduced Zen calligraphy for decoration and favored a simple and natural pottery for his utensils, such as the Bizen style. These ideas were furthered by Takeno Joo (1502–55), a student of Zen from a Sakai merchant family who moved to Kyoto to study tea. Drawn to the aesthetic of *wabi* (rustic simplicity), he was inspired to build a tea room in the manner of the thatched huts used by farmers. Amongst those inspired by the teaching was Sen no Rikyu (1522–91), who codified the ceremony as we know it today. He was also closely connected with Daitoku-ji.

Master of Masters

Rikyu was the son of a wealthy Sakai merchant and from an early age took an interest in the tea ceremony, studying for fifteen years under Takeno Joo. Like his teacher, he was drawn to the study of Zen at Daitoku-ji and he also traveled widely to visit first hand the places where utensils were made, such as the kilns for the pottery. By middle age he had acquired such a reputation that he was appointed tea master to Oda Nobunaga. It was an influential position, for tea was used as a diplomatic tool and alliances were cemented with gifts of expensive utensils. As tea master to the ruler, Rikyu was privy to matters of state.

One of Rikyu's principles was that all should be equal in the tea room, so he dispensed with the niceties of rank and used a small 'crawling entrance' to prevent the wearing of swords and ensure humility in entering. He also promoted the values of *wabi-sabi*, an aesthetic that combines rustic simplicity with natural beauty and an awareness of transience. This was reflected in the utensils he favored, which were made of simple but natural materials. In a similar manner, his tea houses were built in the peasant hut style. His unerring aesthetic sense is captured in an anecdote about his gardener, who had swept the garden free of fallen leaves in keeping with the tea principle of cleanliness. Seeing this, Rikyu completed the scene by shaking a branch and scattering leaves over the path in an irregular manner as ordained by nature. The arrangement of autumn hues was a perfect wabi-sabi presentation for his guests.

Following Nobunaga's death, Rikyu was employed by his successor, Toyotomi Hideyoshi, the only ruler in Japanese

The man who perfected the tea ceremony, Sen no Rikyu, was from the merchant class. His devotion to tea led to him becoming advisor to Japan's rulers, but despite his status he promoted humility, equality and rustic austerity. The *wabi-sabi* aesthetic with which he is associated prizes natural simplicity, irregularity and the patina of age.

history to have risen from the peasant class. While he was eager to learn sophisticated ways, he was also resentful of being made to feel inferior. The ambivalence is captured in an anecdote about a magnificent crop of morning glory Rikyu had cultivated. When Hideyoshi learnt about this, he hurried to see them. Hearing that Hideyoshi was on his way, Rikyu cut down the whole crop. The bewildered Hideyoshi was at a loss,

The darkened atmosphere of the tea room is conducive to intimacy and quiet contemplation, which fosters inner peace. The sense of closeness to nature is enhanced by the simplicity of the materials: soil, wood and paper. Seasonal reference in the utensils serves to further the connection.

but there inside the tea room Rikyu had placed a single dazzling flower. It was a lesson in the aesthetics of minimalism.

The differences between the men are encapsulated in their tea houses. In a typical *nouveau riche* display, Hideyoshi had utensils made of gold for a tea room that was covered all over in gold leaf. By stark contrast, Rikyu's representative tea room, made of earthen walls, paper windows and unpolished beams, was just two tatami mats in size, the bare minimum in which two people could comfortably share the intimacy of a cup of tea.

The tensions between the tea master and his pupil came to a head in 1591, when out of the blue Rikyu was ordered to commit ritual suicide. There has been much speculation about the reason, but it is thought the pretext was the restoration of the Sanmon gate at Daitoku-ji, which Rikyu had funded. A statue of the benefactor was placed on the second floor, along with other images. This enraged Hideyoshi, for it meant that on visits to the temple for tea lessons he would have to pass beneath the 'superior' Rikyu. In revenge, he sought to teach the tea master a very different kind of lesson.

Legacy

The formalities of the modern tea ceremony largely derive from Rikyu, and the precepts he advocated still hold sway: harmony, respect, purity and tranquility. Within this atmosphere are cultivated mindfulness and seasonal awareness. Etiquette is carefully prescribed, and the movements are slow and precise. Utensils are treated as precious objects, to be admired and appreciated (those of historical significance can be immensely valuable). "The way of Tea is a way of salvation through beauty," wrote the philosopher Yanagi Muneyoshi (1889–1961).

During the ceremony there is a Zen-like concern with treasuring the moment, for the ritual is carried out in near silence, creating an atmosphere of heightened awareness. The tea motto of *ichigo ichie* ('just this one time only'), means that each encounter is unique. The implication is that the host will do everything to make the occasion as special as possible, even to the extent of collecting pure spring water from one of Kyoto's hilly streams. Seasonal references in the utensils and the thoughtful selection of decoration are an important part of the preparation, which may also include small touches such as splashing water over the approach to imbue a sense of freshness.

According to Sen no Rikyu, "In Zen, truth is pursued through the discipline of meditation in order to realize enlightenment, while in tea we use training in the procedures to achieve the same end." The spirituality is evident in the peacefulness of the occasion. Time slows down, the external world distances itself, and one is left with the fleeting thoughts of the mind. "By repeating the same polished actions over and over again, fitting yourself into a pattern, you approach the core of yourself," wrote Sen Souoku, a descendant of Rikyu. He is head of one of the three famous tea schools in north Kyoto (Urasenke, Omotesenke and Mushanokojisenke). For 400 years the family lines have continued to prepare, serve and practice tea in the same area of Kyoto, and the Urasenke School has become an international concern with 'embassies' in faraway countries. From its first beginnings in Kyoto's Zen temples, Myoan Eisai's tea has taken seed and spread around the world.

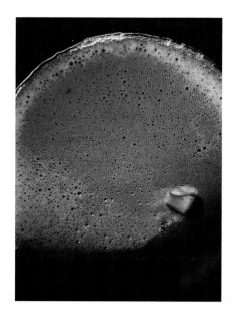

Top At Manpuku-ji, head temple of the Obaku Sect, the tea ceremony is based on the use of tea leaves rather than powder. This is known as *sencha*, which is drunk from cups instead of bowls.
Above The monastical complex of Daitoku-ji is known as 'the home of tea'. Several of its sub-temples have close connections with the tea ceremony, and at Ryogen-in visitors can participate by reserving a day in advance.
Left The aesthetics of the tea ceremony are exemplified by stone water basins, which are simple, natural and bear the patina of age. The rustic charm is accompanied by a constant flow of water, which provides an atmosphere of freshness.

The Sound of Zen:
The Shakuhachi Flute as Spiritual Instrument

Zen, Kyoto and the *shakuhachi* are closely connected. The long bamboo instrument (*shaku* is a unit of length and *hachi* means eight) was first introduced from China in the eighth century and used in ceremonial music known as *gagaku*. Not long afterwards, the music groups were standardized and shakuhachi excluded. The instrument became associated with Buddhism instead, when the head of the powerful Tendai sect, Ennin (794–864), introduced shakuhachi accompaniment to sutra chanting in his Mt Hiei complex.

By the Muromachi period (1333–1573) there had emerged itinerant monk-players called *komoso* who played shakuhachi and begged for a living. (*Komo* refers to their 'straw-mat bedding' and *so* means 'monk'.) The essayist Yoshida Kenko wrote disparagingly of them in *Essays of Idleness* (c. 1330):

Willful and determined, they appear to be devoted to the way of Buddha, but they make strife and quarrel their business. Though dissolute and cruel in appearance they think lightly of death, and cling not at all to life.

Thereafter the straw-mat komoso gravitated into komuso, with the new spelling signifying an identification with Zen (*mu* means 'nothingness'). To the masterless samurai (*ronin*) of the early Edo Era, becoming a shakuhachi itinerant seemed an attractive option, and the komuso swelled in number. It was a time of strict control by the Tokugawa shoguns, and mobility was severely restricted. In return for services to the shogunate, the komuso were not only granted exclusive rights to the shakuhachi but relative freedom to travel. To show their detachment from the world, they wore a *tengai*, a wicker basket that covered head and face. Not all were genuine in their religious devotion. Some acted as government spies and some were more inclined to banditry.

The seventeenth century also saw the emergence of the Fuke Sect, with a focus on *suizen* (blowing Zen) as a counterpart to *zazen* (sitting Zen). The thinking was based on breathing as a means of unity between interior and exterior worlds. As a result, breath was given higher priority than tone. "Do not shrink back from the unclean sound which is caused when the Great Bamboo is blown!" wrote Hisamatsu Fuyo in 1823. On the other hand, by striking the purest of notes, the player might come to realize his true nature: "In one sound, become the Buddha!" ran a saying. The ideal was to become one with the instrument, blowing pure and spontaneously like the wind.

The Fuke Sect had its headquarters at Myoan-ji, a subtemple of Tofuku-ji, and membership was limited to the samurai class. The instrument came to be seen as a means of Zen transmission, ideal for a sect that stressed the non-verbal nature of true understanding. The ethereal tones evoked a sense of spirituality, with the haunting cadences conducive to thoughts of transcendence. Like the violent whacks of the *kyousaku* stick, the sudden shrill sounds of the shakuhachi flute could shock a listener into awakening in more than one sense.

At its peak, the Fuke Sect had eighteen lineages and 140 temples. But such was its reputation for lawlessness that in 1871, following the Meiji Restoration, the sect was outlawed and for a few years the shakuhachi was even banned. Gradually, however, the instrument was reclaimed for secular use, and in Kyoto an association based at Myoan-ji was formed to continue the religious practice (the Fuke Sect was resurrected but now exists more or less in name only).

With the spread overseas of the shakuhachi in modern times, the instrument has become more widely known and even been used in rock music. But for some it remains a spiritual tool rather than a musical device. Because it has no reed, the way of creating pitch and tone are quite distinctive, making it more an extension of the human body than an instrument for producing sound. Breathing, mouth angle, neck movement and fingering are all used to alter pitch, such that the shakuhachi can produce sixty-four tones an octave compared to a mere twelve in the European tradition. One of the concerns is with *tetteion* or 'sound in and of itself,' by which each note is treated in isolation rather than in relation to others. The timbre of a note therefore takes precedence over melody and rhythm, focussing attention on each individual sound. In this way, the practice furthers training in important aspects of Zen, such as mindfulness. More than learning to play music, the shakuhachi player learns to be immersed in 'the now'.

Above The evocative sounds of the *shakuhachi* conjure up the introspective mood of evening and the promise of moonlit illumination.
Opposite above The stone monument inside the entrance of Myoan-ji, the 'shakuhachi subtemple' of Tofuku-ji, bears an inscription saying 'Suizen', or 'Blowing Zen' (as opposed to Sitting Zen).
Right A contemporary shakuhachi player attached to Myoko-ji. In Edo times, *komuso* roamed the land playing the shakuhachi for alms, some of whom also worked as government spies. It led to the Fuke Sect being banned in the Meiji period.

The Taste of Zen:
Kyoto Temple Cuisine

Shojin ryori is a special kind of Zen food that originated in monasteries for ceremonial occasions. Once it was only served to the guests of monks, but nowadays it is available to the general public (Daitoku-ji and Tenryu-ji have specialist restaurants). It is vegetarian in keeping with monastic precepts, which state that the taking of animal life is forbidden. It is also local, organic and seasonal, making it not only healthy but environmentally sound.

The normal fare of Zen monasteries is based on the principle of frugality and the suppression of desire. The regime was codified by Eihei Dogen (1200–53), also called Dogen Zenji, in a remarkable tract entitled *Tenzo Kyoku* (Instructions for the Cook), which prescribes the exact way in which food should be prepared. Avoidance of waste, selection of the freshest ingredients and cultivation of mindfulness are advocated. In this way, the creation of a dish becomes a sacred task, turning it from domestic chore to spiritual practice. The position of cook thus assumed a special place in the monastic community and "You are what you eat" was taken seriously. In fact, much of the healthiest Japanese food originated in monasteries: miso, *natto* (fermented beans), tofu, *umeboshi* (pickled plum) and *takuan* (pickled radish).

The refined style of Zen food known as *shojin ryori* had already come into existence by the thirteenth century. *Ryori* means 'cooking' and *shojin* consists of two Chinese characters: *sho* meaning 'purify' and *jin* meaning 'advance' or 'progress'. The name thus suggests that the food promotes purity in body and mind, advancing spiritual progress. It was based on the characteristics Dogen advocated, with mindful preparation and high-quality ingredients. In addition, aesthetic considerations were taken into account, such as the food being arranged according to seasonal colors. The meal became more than just a treat for the palate; it was a feast for the eyes.

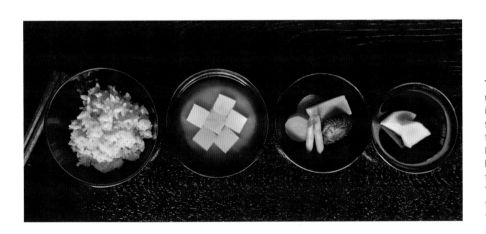

Top Grains of rice donated by monks are left out for birds in keeping with the spirit of selflessness and compassion for fellow creatures.
Left A typical Zen meal is based on 'one soup, one dish', together with rice and pickles. The food is eaten from a set of four bowls in portions that are 'just enough'.

Amongst the many vegetarian dishes served at Shigetsu, a *shojin ryori* restaurant in Tenryu-ji, is grilled eggplant with sweet miso. Courses consist of rice, soup and a number of seasonal dishes. Reservations are required in advance for two or more people.

Along with vegetables, foodstuffs may include beans, seeds, nuts, mushrooms, wild herbs and roots. Seasoning is designed to bring out the natural taste, with typical ingredients being salt, sugar, soy sauce and seaweed with vinegar. Subtle tastes are preferred, with strong flavors such as onion and garlic avoided altogether. Preparation is based on Chinese principles, with the sole implements being a strainer, grater and pestle and mortar. Consideration is given to balance and health. In summer, yin substances such as lotus root or tomato are used to cool the body, and in winter yang elements like ginger to warm the body. The Five Elements theory means that there are five methods of cooking, five tastes and five colors of food. There are Five Reflections, too, to be chewed over before eating: appreciation of the food; consideration of one's worthiness; also of one's purity; the medicinal value; and gratitude.

Meals served to tourists these days remain based on Zen values. The contents differ from season to season, and the number of dishes varies according to price. Typically, there might be a selection of boiled food, such as Ingen bean, carrot, pumpkin, mangetout and *yuba* (tofu skin). Alongside this might be mashed ginan nuts with plum sauce, and a small dish of pickles such as daikon radish and cucumber. There will also be a vinegared dish, such as wax gourd (also known as winter melon). This will all be served with rice and soup, for example, bamboo rice and red miso soup containing tofu, seaweed and Japanese parsley. Because of the emphasis on sourcing local produce, shojin ryori in Kyoto is typified by the quality of its tofu products,

which draw on the fresh spring water underlying the city. It is also characterized by the use of *kyoyasai* (Kyoto vegetables special to the prefecture, such as distinctive carrots and radish).

The 'flagship food' of Zen food is *gomadofu* (sesame tofu). Not only is it particularly delicious but grinding the sesame mindfully in *seiza* position is considered an early morning exercise that acts as mental preparation for the coming day. The sesame seeds are soaked in pure water the night before, then ground for a full hour. Given this kind of preparation, it seems only proper to consume the food with due gratitude, and the Japanese way is to put the hands together before eating and say "Itadakimasu" (I humbly receive). In this way, the meal becomes something more than mere food, but a form of participation in an ancient tradition. In Zen, as elsewhere, a healthy body makes for a healthy mind.

The entrance to the Shigetsu restaurant has a *noren* cloth with brushed ink circle, a symbol in Zen of perfection and enlightenment.

Enso circles, such as this by Gensho Hozumi (b. 1937), are prized works of art that carry the artist's personal seal.

Picturing Zen:
Temple Painting and Brushwork

The arrival of Zen had a great impact on the development of art in Japan, for the concern with "direct pointing at the heart of things" brought an emphasis on inner truth. Simplicity and minimalism were the watchwords. The favored medium was the imported ink painting of China, with the black and white expressive of unified opposites. Idealized mountain scenes showed people dwarfed by their surrounds and integrated into their environment. In this way, the human ego was shown to be relatively insignificant.

In the fifteenth century, an important school of art was initiated at Shokoku-ji by a Chinese immigrant called Josetsu (1405–96), later dubbed 'the father of ink painting'. His lineage passed via Shobun to the greatest practitioner of all, Sesshu Toyo (1420–1506), and in the process developed from the copying of Chinese models to the creation of a specifically Japanese style. Along with such traits as naturalness and tranquility was the conscious use of empty space. Thanks to the artist-monks of Shokoku-ji, Japan witnessed a golden age of ink painting.

One of the genres to be invigorated by Zen was portrait painting (*chinzo*). Because the sect places emphasis on direct transmission, the teacher plays a vital role and portraits of revered masters are highly treasured. The convention is for the elderly monks to be robed and seated cross-legged on an abbot's chair, with slippers neatly placed before them. The subjects are portrayed truthfully with 'warts and all', as a result of which there is great individuality. At Tofuku-ji, a huge portrait of founder Enni Ben'en depicts him as a frail old man with grumpy expression and lazy eye. On the other hand, a famous portrait of Ikkyu Sojun shows him looking askance with stern expression,

'Circle-Square-Triangle' are thought to be the fundamental building blocks of the universe. The concept can be traced back to ancient India and was popularized in Zen by the Edo-era artist-monk Sengai Gibon (1750–1837).

as if questioning the integrity of the observer.

Another notable genre is Nehan-zu, which illustrates the passage of Shakyamuni into nirvana. The pictures are exhibited on the anniversary of his death (February 15) and follow a set pattern, with the dying Buddha portrayed in a grove of trees under a full moon surrounded by mourners and grieving animals. The largest of the pictures is at Tofuku-ji, painted in 1408, and is an astonishing fifteen yards in length.

The most striking temple paintings feature the unmistakable face of Bodhidharma, known in Japan as Daruma. Traditionally, he is shown with bald head, bushy eyebrows, round face and glaring eyes. The intimidating fierceness serves as a model of determination, and there is a particularly fine example at Nanzen-ji, painted by Shokei (late fifteenth century), which shows the patriarch with overhanging eyebrows and spiky hairs sticking out of nose and ears.

Temples host a number of Zen sayings and pronouncements rendered in calligraphic form. The formal entrance to Kennin-ji provides an example in a standing screen bearing four Chinese characters which say 'First Zen cave' (i.e. temple).

Calligraphy

The arrival of Zen also proved an invigorating force for the ancient art of calligraphy. Copying sutra, which was thought to imprint the sacred words on the mind, was used to further focused concentration. Rather than straining to make greater effort, the Zen practitioner seeks to relax and empty the mind so that the writer becomes one with the writing. Emphasis is put on the 'nowness' of the moment, and brushed script by a Zen priest (*bokuseki*), sometimes available for a fee at temples, is valued for its spiritual quality, with the aim being to capture in a single breath writing expressive of 'no-mind'.

The use of wall hangings with Zen sayings (*zengo*), sometimes accompanied by illustrations, was introduced to tea ceremonies in the fifteenth century and thereafter became a popular form of decoration. "Everyday is a blessing"; "No thoughts, no desires"; "The Way lies in a peaceful heart" are examples of such Zen sayings. The personal character of the calligraphy means that the writing is often unreadable, showing the individualism of a sect concerned with inner exploration. It reflects also the intuitive nature of Zen, by transforming the verbal into the visual.

The Edo period (1600–1868) saw the emergence of Zenga inspired by Hakuin Ekaku (1686–1768) and his followers. The paintings they produced were simple, direct and full of life. Some illustrate *koan* riddles or moral lessons, accompanied by calligraphy, while others depict Buddha images or Mt Fuji. A particularly popular subject was the symbolic circle, known as *enso*, which represents oneness or the essential unity of things. A closed circle suggests the striving for perfection, while an open circle allows for further development. Carried out in one fluid stroke, the brushwork typifies the Zen inclination to immediacy and spontaneity.

For temple visitors, the most impressive of all the artwork is often the ceiling dragon found in Lecture Halls (Hatto or Hodo). The mythical dragon, which originated in China, comprises parts of different animals whose attributes it assumes. Thus it has the mouth of a crocodile, the horn of a deer, the body of a carp, the talons of a falcon, the body of a snake, etc. Since the creatures inhabit watery depths, they are thought to guard against fire, while at the same time are able to fly up to heaven. As a Kennin-ji pamphlet puts it, in this way they combine water and wisdom, thereby sending "the nourishing rain of the teachings of Buddhism down onto followers".

Capturing the Moment:
Haiku and Zen Poetry

The relationship of Zen to haiku has been much disputed. Commentators such as R. H. Blyth and D. T. Suzuki claimed that the short verse was inextricably tied to the spirit of Zen. Yet, as a form of poetry, haiku can be written by anyone regardless of religion, and some of the greatest practitioners have had no ties to Zen. Of the 'four great haiku poets', Kobayashi Issa was a Pure Land believer (Jodo Shinshu) and Masaoka Shiki an agnostic. On the other hand, it would be impossible to deny that Zen has played a vital role in shaping the salient characteristics of the genre.

During the Muromachi period (1333–1573), when Zen was an important cultural force, priests such as Shotetsu and Ikkyu Sojun produced poetry that was direct, imaginative and profound:

And what is it, the heart?
It is the sound of the pine breeze
in the ink painting

It was some time, however, before haiku emerged. It had its roots in Japanese traditional poetry, notably the short poems known as *tanka* which have a 5–7–5–7–7 syllable pattern. At poetry gatherings, the form was adopted for contests of linked verse (*renga*), with the first 5–7–5 being responded to by another poet. Over time, the seventeen syllables became an independent verse of their own.

The perfection of haiku as an art form was largely due to the inspirational figure of Matsuo Basho (1644–94), who raised the verse from mere poetic pastime. It is thought that in his youth he studied Zen in Kyoto while training in poetry under Kigin Kitamura. Later, when he revisited the city, he stayed at the Zen temple of Konpuku-ji. After moving to Edo (now Tokyo), the poet studied Zen for a year and a half with the priest Butcho and thereafter hovered on the edge of the sect, wearing monk's clothes but never actually becoming one (he blamed his devotion to haiku for the lack of religious self-discipline).

Under the influence of Basho, haiku took on the attributes with which we are familiar today: a seasonal reference; the juxtaposition of divergent images; profundity

Carved into a large stone at Entsu-ji is a haiku written by the early twentieth-century master Kyoshi Takahama. "Stepping on/Fallen persimmon leaves/A visit to Entsu-ji."

Just as photography aims to capture the perfect moment with a camera, so haiku aims to capture the moment in words. The juxtaposition of contrasting elements brings suggestiveness and depth.

within brevity. It also took on some of the traits of Zen, such as a favoring of intuition; observation rather than explanation; self-effacement rather than assertion; and an 'ah' moment of realization. It is said that truly great haiku are composed when the poet is in a state of 'no-mind', enabling a direct expression of nature.

Something of these qualities can be found in Basho's most well-known haiku. On one level it seems a simple nature poem, capturing the moment that a frog goes 'plop' into the water.

The old pond;
A frog jumps in
The sound of water

On a symbolic level, the stillness of the pond is disturbed by the frog in just the same way as the mind in *zazen* sitting meditation is disturbed by thought. However, if the observer waits patiently, the pond-mind will inevitably resume its stillness. But what if the sound of the frog represents a moment of enlightenment, and the immersion in water signifies oneness with the universe? It is as if in one single sound the frog penetrates surface reality to realize the Buddha-nature that connects us all. In this way, hidden depths are opened up, and the 'elegant profundity' of the poem lies not so much in what is said as what is unsaid.

A hundred years after Basho, an ardent admirer of his became a resident of Kyoto. Yosa Buson (1716–84) was not only a poet but also a celebrated painter and many of his haiku have a strong pictorial bent. He took an interest in Zen and out of devotion to his predecessor he restored the hut at Konpuku-ji where Basho once stayed. He held poetry gatherings there and it was the place he chose for his grave.

When I die
bury me close to his monument—
withered pampas grass

In modern times, haiku has spread to the West through translations by such eminent figures as R. H. Blyth, J. Hackett and Harold Henderson. Among the first to try their hand at English-language haiku was Ezra Pound with *In a Station of the Metro* (1913). Since then, other poets have followed in his footsteps, notably the Beat Generation of Jack Kerouac, William S. Burroughs and Allen Ginsberg who helped popularize the genre. Several modern practitioners have also had strong Kyoto Zen connections, notably Gary Snyder, Kenneth Rexroth, Cyd Corman and Edith Shiffert. Under their influence, the single lines of Chinese characters have been transformed into horizontal haiku in English of three lines. For writers around the world, it has now become regular practice to try and capture the moment—the haiku moment.

(For more on haiku, see Konpuku-ji, page 142.)

The Discipline of No-Mind:
Zen and the Martial Arts

From its very beginnings, Zen in Japan was associated with the warrior class. Samurai and monk cherished similar values: fortitude, persistence, frugality, suppression of the ego and training for death. Both strove for mastery of the self and both valued discipline. Moreover, both were concerned with the sharpening of awareness and a focus on 'the now'. As a result, spiritual practice came to be used for martial training. Sitting *zazen* was seen as a means of intensifying concentration, while at the same time training the practitioner in endurance and overcoming discomfort. In this way, Zen was seen as offering useful skills for martial arts, and it influenced judo, karate and particularly the forms of *kendo* and *kyudo*.

During the Warring States period in Japan (1467–1568), when central authority broke down, it was common for regional warlords to take Zen priests as advisors. As well as giving spiritual training, the priests sometimes acted as military advisors and negotiators. The great unifiers of Japan—Nobunaga, Hideyoshi and Ieyasu—all had Zen confidants, and it was at this time that the great ideologue of martial arts emerged, Takuan Soho (1573–1645).

Born into a samurai household in present-day Hyogo, Takuan entered religious training as a young boy and came to Daitoku-ji when he was nineteen. He was appointed abbot at thirty-six, but soon left to travel and collect funds for the temple's renovation. Like other Zen masters of the period, Takuan was proficient in a wide range of arts, among them calligraphy, painting, poetry and the tea ceremony. His versatility extended to *budo* (martial arts), including *kenjutsu* in which sticks were used for sword practice.

Below and bottom A participant bows before a sword prior to a contest in *Iaido* (sword fighting). Respect for the weapon is an integral part of martial arts, as is correctness of form and etiquette. The long grip of the *katana* (traditional sword) is shaped so as to accommodate the use of both hands. Demonstrations of martial arts are held at temples and shrines throughout the year, indicative of their religious connections.

THE ART OF KYUDO

Kyudo (Japanese archery) first developed as a martial art during the Kamakura period (1187–1333) and thereafter became a common form of training for samurai. It differs from *kendo* archery in that there is a stationary rather than a moving target, and since the merest distraction can affect the outcome of a shot, the archer needs a focused mind. Whereas in kendo one has to confront an opponent, kyudo is more about confronting oneself. If an arrow fails to hit the target, the archer is forced to reflect on technique and mental application. Since this requires intensifying concentration, kyudo has looked to Zen for training. Indeed, it is known as *ritsuzen* (standing meditation) as opposed to *zazen* (sitting meditation).

In Edo times, kyudo was particularly popular as a means of developing mental power, and its legacy is evident at the popular Toshiya (archery competition) at Sanjusangendo, held each January when some 2,000 participants gather from across Japan. It remained a leading martial art throughout Meiji times, and In the years leading up to World War II it was a compulsory physical education class in Japanese schools.

In the postwar years, kyudo spread to the West through the immensely popular *Zen in the Art of Archery* (1948 in German, 1953 in English). The author, Eugen Herrigel, had taught philosophy at a university in Sendai for six years, and because of his interest in mysticism had studied kyudo with a master called Awa Kenzo who, contrary to other instructors, put great stress on spirituality. On one occasion, in pitch darkness, he not only managed to hit the bull but fired a second shot which splintered the shaft of the first arrow. "Only when one turns oneself into the target can one start walking the path of Zen," he stated. Though the book remains controversial, it inspired a whole generation and initiated a genre of sports books dealing with the 'inner game'. From its early days of samurai and swordsmanship, kyudo had hit the mark in the West too.

Kyudo master Hiroaki Kato performs the ceremonial opening of Kyoto's annual Toshiya competition by firing the first arrow. The contest takes place at Sanjusangendo on the second Sunday of January and features 2,000 archers from around the country. Unlike in European archery, the bow string is pulled back all the way to the ear.

A sword fighting contest held at Shiramine Shrine in the north of Kyoto. Martial arts in Japan draw upon the Shinto tradition as well as the discipline of Zen.

Amongst the people Takuan advised was Yagyu Munenori (1571–1646), a *daimyo* and kendo instructor to the shogun. Munenori is remembered as the founder of Yagyu Shinkage-ryu, and he wrote a treatise on Zen and swordsmanship, *The Sword and the Mind*.... "It is the very mind itself that leads men astray; Of the mind, do not be mindless," he wrote. Upon Munenori's recommendation, Tokugawa Iemitsu took Takuan as his Zen master and he even had a temple specially built so that as abbot Takuan would be on hand for consultation.

Among the writings Takuan left behind is *The Unfettered Mind*, consisting of two long letters and an essay in which the spirit of Zen is applied to sword fighting. The treatise considers how the swordsman may become unified with his unconscious self as well as the difference between selfless and selfish motives. Most importantly, Takuan puts forward the concept of *mushin* (no-mind), a state of awareness emptied of distracting thought:

Don't fix your mind on anything when facing an opponent. If you hold on anything, your free motions will be disturbed by your fixed mind. And your opponent will find an unguarded moment to attack. Victory or defeat is decided in an instant. Therefore you must not fix your mind anywhere, and must pay attention to all places with complete consciousness. This state of attention everywhere without thinking and feeling is called *mushin*. It is the state of complete awareness.

Takuan's thinking was to have a profound effect on kendo and sword fighting. Miyamoto Musashi, for instance, author of *The Book of Five Rings* (1645), may have taken instruction from him at Daitoku-ji and later wrote: "Confronting an opponent, I forget life and death. Staying in *mushin* and trusting whatever happens, I am free from limitations, observing what disturbs me."

Kyoto

2 km
10000 ft

N

TAKAO

Genko-an 24

Daisen-in
Koto-in 17 15 Daitoku-ji
Zuiho-in 16 13
26 14
Kinkaku-ji
Ryoan-ji 28 Ryogen-in
Toji-in 22 Shokoku-ji 25

Saga-
Arashiyama
Uzumasa 20 Shunko-in
Taizo-in 19 18 Myoshin-ji
Hanazono Emmachi

Nijo

21
Tenryu-ji

Saiho-ji (Kokedera) 23

Nishioji

Tambaguchi

San'in Main Line

Karasuma Line

Kyoto Station

Hankyu Arashiyama Line

Katsuragawa

Tokaido Shinkansen

Tofukuji

Inari

Funda-in
(Sesshu-ji)

Nara Line

JR-
Fujinomori

Momoyama

Entsu-ji 34

Eizan Line

Enko-ji 30
Shisendo 31
Konpuku-ji 35

Kanga-an 33

Ginkaku-ji 27

Tenju-an
Konchi-in 12 11 9 Nanzen-ji
10 Nanzen-in

GION
Entoku-in
1 2 3
Kennin-ji Kodai-ji

Tozai Line

Yamashina

Reiun-in 7
5 Tofuku-ji
6
8 Komyo-in

Keifuku
Cable Line

Hieizan
Cable Line

Keihan Ishiyama Sakamoto line

Karas

Otsukyo

Otsu

Tokaido Main Line

Tokaido Shinkansen

Tozai Line

Rokujizo

Kohata

Obaku

Manpuku-ji 32

UJI
CITY

Uji

4 Kosho-ji

Keihan Uji Line

Kintetsu Kyoto Line

IR-
Ogura

Shinden

Shin

JOYO
CITY

Joyo

Nara Line

Nagaike

UJITAWARA
TOWN

Yamashiro-
Aodani

Yamashiro-
Taga

IDE TOWN

HIRAKATA
CITY

Katamachi Line

Tanabe-nishi
IC

Shuon-an (Ikkyu-ji) 29
KYOTANABE
CITY

Hozukyo

Kyoto's Main Zen Temples

Kyoto's Zen Temples

KENNIN-JI 建仁寺
Kyoto's Oldest Zen Temple
FOUNDED 1202

Kennin-ji is the oldest Zen temple in Kyoto. It was founded by a monk called Myoan Eisai (1141–1215), who brought the new teaching from China, and it houses some outstanding artwork. But perhaps the most remarkable feature is its location in Gion, Kyoto's largest geisha district, where it is neighbor to drinking bars and entertainment establishments. The proximity of worldly and otherworldly pursuits has long characterized Japanese religion, meaning that temple tea rooms stand alongside geisha tea houses. The restrained communing of one is offset by the bibulous chit-chat of the other. The floating world of Buddhism here merges with that of 'the water trade' and, as the wits have it, paradise can be found on either side of the temple wall.

Most visitors enter Kennin-ji from the north, though the layout is seen to best effect by approaching from the south, starting with the Imperial Messenger's Gate (Chakushimon). It is the temple's oldest structure, for Kennin-ji was often

The Choun-tei Garden at Kennin-ji has three central rocks representing the historical Buddha and two bodhisattva attendants. Behind them can be seen contemporary *fusuma* panels portraying Vietnamese landscapes by *katazome* stencil dyeing artist Mika Toba, created for the temple's 800th anniversary.

The classic Daio-en, or Grand Garden, at Kennin-ji features raked white sand lined by dark moss and rocks in a yin–yang balancing. This is furthered by the two contrasting 'islands', whereby a round flat Turtle Island is offset by the vertical Crane Island beyond it. In the background is a fine Karamon (Chinese gate) with curved roof, known as the 'helmet style' for its resemblance to a warrior's headgear.

Subtemples and Indian Deities

The foundation of Kennin-ji was a huge undertaking, which took three years to complete. Named after the era in which it was built, it boasted extensive grounds and at one point had as many as fifty-three subtemples. Now there are just fourteen, most of which are closed except for special openings. Ryosoku-in, a subtemple in the northeast of the complex, houses a Bishamonten shrine open to the public and hosts *zazen* sitting meditation for laypeople. The deity is a guardian of the north, one of a group of Hindu protectors incorporated into Buddhism. Another is the female deity Marishiten (Marici), housed at Zenkyo-an in the southwest. She is associated with the sun and was popular with samurai who, by binding her protective power to themselves, trusted that her image would dazzle their enemies into defeat. Her animal messenger is the wild boar, which explains why statues of the creature are so abundant at the subtemple.

The shrines to Indian deities at Ryosoku-in and Zenkyo-an are complemented by a small Shinto shrine on the eastern side of Kennin-ji which houses a tutelary *kami*, protector of the spirit of place. It is indicative of the open-mindedness of Zen. Also of note is the memorial to Eihei Dogen, founder of Soto Zen. He first came to study at Kennin-ji shortly after Eisai's death, from 1217 to 1223. He went to further his studies in China, then again resided at the temple from 1228 to 1230 before leaving to

devastated by fire (the last rebuilding was 250 years ago). Stand in front of the gate looking north and you can see straight down the central axis, passing over the lotus pond bridge through the Sanmon gate to the Hatto (Lecture Hall) and beyond that, the Hojo (Abbot's Quarters).

The grounds are not as grand as at other monasteries but are none the less distinguished by the use of neatly trimmed tea bushes. This is in reference to the temple founder, Myoan Eisai, who brought back seeds from China and promoted tea for its medicinal purposes. He lies buried in the Founder's Hall, near which stands a large memorial stone commemorating the introduction of tea (Eisai called it 'a miraculous elixir'). On April 20 each year, the anniversary of his death, the temple hosts here a large tea ceremony.

start his own temple. One could say therefore that Kennin-ji was in a way mother temple to both Rinzai and Soto. The formation of the two Zen sects was part of a wider fragmentation in religion that followed from the new social order instigated by Japan's first samurai-led government in 1185.

Matchless Artworks

The grounds of Kennin-ji, while spacious, may not be as inspiring as at other great monasteries, but the Abbot's Quarters (Hojo) at the heart of the complex contain an almost matchless wealth of artwork. Laid out around the buildings are a variety of gardens, the most celebrated of which contains a triad of rocks representing Buddha and two attendants. A sixteenth-century tea house is considered the finest of its type, and there are paintings by the top artists of the day.

Myoan Eisai (1141–1215)

The Founder of Rinzai in Japan and the Apostle of Tea

Portrait of Myoan Eisai, founder of Kennin-ji. The style of portrait, called *chinzo*, shows the abbot in ceremonial robes seated in a large chair with folded legs and slippers laid out before him. Such portraits were used as a means of Dharma transmission.

Myoan Eisai (also known as Yosai) was born into a Shinto household as son of a priest at Kibitsu Jinja in Okayama. He was sent away early to study Buddhism, and at the young age of fourteen was ordained into the Tendai sect. He twice made the perilous boat trip to China, once in 1158 to deepen his understanding of Tendai and a second time in 1187 with the purpose of traveling on to India. Instability in Central Asia prevented this, however, and instead he studied for four years with a Chan master.

On his return, Eisai attempted to propagate the new teaching but was faced with hostility from the established sects, particularly Tendai to which he belonged. The notion of direct transmission outside the scriptures threatened their scholarship. There was widespread belief at the time in *mappo*, an age of degeneration in Buddhist teaching thought to have begun in 1050, and Eisai saw Zen as a useful means of combatting the effects and revitalizing the moribund monasteries of Japan.

Eisai's first temple was at Shofuku-ji in Hakata, but because of resistance to his teaching he went to the seat of the warrior class in Kamakura, where he argued that Zen would be good for Japan, for by suppressing the ego it would promote greater peace and harmony. For their part, the authorities saw the new religion as a way of combatting the established sects of Tendai and Shingon, along with their imperial connections. With the backing of Minamoto Yoritomo, first of the Kamakura shoguns, Eisai was able to set up a temple there called Jufuku-ji.

Following Yoritomo's death in 1199, Eisai won the support of the new shogun for the establishment of a large monastery in Kyoto. For pragmatic reasons, Kennin-ji remained part of the Tendai sect, only officially becoming Zen after Eisai's time. Amongst his publications was *Drink Tea and Prolong Life* (1214), and his promotion of tea as an antidote to falling asleep during *zazen* did much to secure its place in monastery life. Eisai thus has claims not only to have sewn the seeds of Zen in Japan but those of the tea ceremony too.

Above Irregularity is a key element in Japanese gardens, with stepping stones carefully chosen to give a sense of flow. They are placed closely together to allow for the small steps of those in kimono, and appreciation of the aesthetics involved is part of the pleasure of the approach.
Opposite Kennin-ji's ceiling painting of twin dragons is unorthodox in that the creature is usually depicted singly within a circle representing the universe. The dragon's watery aspect serves as a protective charm against fire, while its combinatory nature makes it a symbol of the cosmic life force. The black ink *sumi-e* image here was installed in 2002 to mark Kennin-ji's 800th anniversary (previously it had been the only Kyoto monastery without a ceiling dragon).

The temple's chief pride is a large painting of the Wind and Thunder Gods by the early seventeenth-century artist Tawaraya Sotatsu (the original is in the Kyoto National Museum). Also of note are wall hangings by master artist Kaiho Yusho and Chinese-style *fusuma* paintings by the twentieth-century Kyoto artist Kansetsu Hashimoto, whose Daoist scenes are a reminder of the sect's origins.

Along with these traditional art forms are the bold colors of contemporary dye artist Mika Toba. In this refashioning of the Zen spirit, the age-old *katazome* style (stencil dyeing using rice glue) is given a distinctly modern feel. Bold and large scale (across eight panels), the scenes of Vietnamese waterscapes are dramatically realistic, yet in their suggestion of ebb and flow they have universal themes that reference those of Hashimoto.

The modern take on traditional aesthetics is also seen to stunning effect in the nearby Lecture Hall (Hatto), which features an astonishing ceiling painting of twin dragons (visitors sometimes lie on the floor to fully appreciate it). Commissioned in 2002, it was painted in Hokkaido on a huge piece of Japanese paper by Junsaku Koizumi. Ceiling dragons are traditionally painted singly inside a circle representing the universe. Here, however, the two dragons sprawl across the whole width of the ceiling, as if unable to be contained. Like temple guardians, one dragon has an open mouth while the mouth of the other is closed, voicing the mystic *A-un* (Aum) which signifies the beginning and end of all things. In their reconciliation of opposites, the twin dragons thus transcend division and serve as a model of life's underlying unity.

KENNIN-JI AT A GLANCE

Founded 1202 by Myoan Eisai (aka Yosai); founding patron Minamoto Yoriie. 'Temple of the Kennin Era'

Affiliation Head of the Kennin-ji School of Rinzai Zen (14 subtemples, 70 branch temples)

Special features Wind and Thunder Gods, Twin Dragons ceiling, dry landscape gardens, artwork in the Hojo

Opening 10 am–4.30 pm; 4 pm in winter; Hatto and Hojo (¥500); sutra copying (¥1000)

Access 10 mins from Gion Shijo Station, Keihan line; 5 mins from Yasaka Shrine

Events Apr 8: Hanamatsuri for Buddha's birthday; Apr 20: Yotsugashira tea event; Dec 31: numbered tickets to ring New Year bell

Zazen 2nd Sunday, except Aug: meditation and talk in Japanese 8–10 am; 9–11 am in winter (¥300 donation). 2 day *sesshin* early Aug. Also *zazen* by reservation at Ryosoku-in (¥1000) (details in Japanese: http://ryosokuin.com/)

Contact 075 561 6363 (www.kenninji.jp/english/)

This monument was erected by the specialist tea shop Gion Tsujiri, founded in 1860. Behind is a garden with thirty tea trees brought in recent times from Guoqing Temple in China, where Eisai studied Zen. Each year on June 5, the anniversary of his death, powdered tea from the plants is offered to his memory at the Founder's Hall.

The Gods of Wind and Thunder (Fujin and Raijin) were painted by Tawaraya Sotatsu in the early seventeenth century. The depiction on gold foil highlights the two bustling figures, whose energy spills over the edges of the screen leaving the central panels as a prime example of *ma* (the aesthetic of empty space). As with most temple paintings these days, a digital copy is displayed (the original is in the Kyoto National Museum).

ENTOKU-IN 圓徳院
Elegant Gardens and Artwork
FOUNDED 1605

The south garden of the Abbot's Quarters features calm 'water' edged by small rocks evocative of a river delta. The effect is a standard feature known as *araiso*, or rocky shore. The garden, which was created for Nene's more formal guests, has a subdued feeling.

Entoku-in is a subtemple of Kodai-ji, which is where Nene, the widow of the feudal lord Toyotomi Hideyoshi, spent the last years of her life. With its narrow corridors, sliding screens and rock gardens, it is a fascinating small world of prized cultural assets with a surprise around every corner. It is particularly popular in autumn for the stunning illumination of maple leaves, but for much of the rest of the year it is often overlooked for its more famous mother temple of Kodai-ji.

The entrance gate is worth noting as it is in the style of a samurai house. There is a raked gravel garden in front of the main hall, but the main item of interest here are the sliding screen paintings. The subtle black and white landscape by master artist Hasegawa Tohaku contrasts with modern creations in which traditional subjects like moon, pine, plum blossom and bamboo are depicted in bright colors.

The pride of the subtemple lies at the end of the route, which leads along a narrow corridor around the wooden building. This is a magnificent rock garden built by the famed designer Kobori Enshu some 400 years ago. It is in the ornate Momoyama style, with flamboyance rather than restraint to the fore. A vigorous dry river passes amongst a profusion of rocks, donated by samurai from around the country. A green tea set is served on the veranda, from where visitors ponder the groupings of vertical and horizontal rocks and the arrangement of different shapes and colors.

The subtemple offers the rare chance of a 'tea ceremony' in an authentic tea room. This involves squeezing through a small 'crawling' entrance into an enclosed world of *wabi-sabi* elegance. There is room for four or five people, and reservations are required a day ahead (before 4 pm). Here, as the tea is whisked with mindful deliberation, one can sit, sip and taste the very essence of Zen.

The north garden, for informal occasions, features a dynamic dry landscape which is illuminated to spectacular effect during cherry blossom and maple seasons. The array of striking rocks were donated to Nene by samurai from around the country.

ENTOKU-IN AT A GLANCE

Founded 1605 by Toyotomi Hideyoshi's widow Nene. 'Subtemple of Perfect Virtue'

Affiliation Kennin-ji School of Rinzai Zen

Special features Rock gardens, *fusuma* paintings, tea ceremony (¥1500)

Opening 10 am–5 pm (¥500)

Event Late autumn: maple leaf illumination (–9.30 pm)

Access City bus 206 Higashiyama-Yasui stop

Contact (075) 525-0101

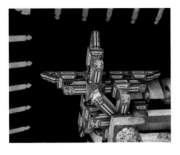

KODAI-JI 高台寺
A Widow's Refined Retreat
FOUNDED 1605

Kodai-ji is one of Kyoto's top tourist attractions, boasting sumptuous grounds and a wealth of Important Cultural Assets. It was founded by the widow of pre-eminent feudal lord, warrior and politician Toyotomi Hideyoshi in memory of her late husband. Following his death in 1598, she became a nun as was the custom. Known popularly as Nene (1546–1624), she bore the honorary title of Kodai-in and won the favor of the new shogun, Tokugawa Ieyasu. The temple thus has a lavish touch, noted for its connections with the tea ceremony and for the use of gold-embossed 'Kodai-ji lacquer'. These days, the temple also has a reputation for its illuminations, which take place in spring (cherry blossom) and autumn (maple leaves), when dazzling images are reflected in shallow ponds.

The Main Hall was once covered in lacquer and gold, but after burning down in 1912 it was rebuilt in plain wood. The raked gravel garden is more elaborate than is usual, reflecting Nene's guiding hand. The grounds are dominated by a stroll garden credited to master designer Kobori Enshu, with an upper and lower pond particularly beautiful in autumn. The refinement is encapsulated by a moon-viewing platform that has a cypress bark roof obscuring sight of the sky. Viewers were invited instead to look down at the moon's reflection passing over the surface of the pond. It calls to mind the words of Eihei Dogen: "Enlightenment is like the moon reflected on the water. The moon does not get wet, nor is the water broken."

The Founder's Hall houses a statue of Sanko Joeki, the Kennin-ji abbot who took over the running of the temple after Nene's death. Here too can be seen examples of the Kodai-ji lacquerwork with insets in gold. The ceiling is noteworthy for being partly covered with panels taken from Hideyoshi's private boat and partly with wood from Nene's ox-cart. A covered corridor leads from the building up the slope to a Memorial Hall named Otamaya, which has lifelike statues of Hideyoshi and Nene, the latter of whom lies buried beneath the altar looking south towards her husband's grave.

The path continues up the hillside to two historic tea houses dating back to the sixteenth century, which were relocated from the ruined Fushimi Castle. One has a striking roof shaped like the spokes of a bamboo umbrella, while the other, unusually, has two

KODAI-JI AT A GLANCE

Founded 1605 by Toyotomi Hideyoshi's wife Nene; founding priest Sanko Joeki. 'Temple of Kodai-in' (honorary name of Nene)

Affiliation Kennin-ji School of Rinzai Zen

Special features Memorial Hall, Founder's Hall, Main Hall, gardens, tea houses; Entoku-in subtemple

Opening 9 am–5 pm (¥600)

Events Spring and autumn illumination; late June–early Sept: Jinchu-seki tea ceremony to honor Hideyoshi (¥5500); Sept (weekends) moon-viewing (¥6000)

Access Bus 207, 206 to Higashiyama Yasui, 5 mins walk. Taxi from Kyoto Station 15 mins.

Contact (075) 561-9966 (www.kodaiji.com)

stories. They were assembled here in honor of Hideyoshi, who was a keen practitioner of tea, and the hillside site offers views over the city as well as of a massive statue of Ryozen Kannon, built next door in 1955 as a war memorial.

One imagines that the open stretch of nature, adorned by a delightful bamboo grove, offset any sense that the widowed Nene might have had of being 'cloistered'. She belonged to the Soto sect but had a personal connection to the Rinzai abbot of Kennin-ji, to whom she bequeathed her temple. Although there is no one in residence these days, priests from the main temple continue to visit daily to perform rituals and keep her memory alive. Of all the Zen temples in Kyoto, it is said that Kodai-ji has the most feminine atmosphere, and still today it remains a place of refinement with exclusive tea ceremonies and moon-viewing parties.

Right The seventeenth-century Iho-an, Cottage of Lingering Fragrance, belonged to a wealthy merchant whose lover was the renowned beauty Yoshino Tayu. It is one of several prized tea houses at the temple.

Opposite top Ornamental detail on the Memorial Hall for Hideyoshi and Nene (whose formal name is Kita no Mandokoro). The bright colors typify the flamboyance of the Momoyama era when the country enjoyed the fruits of unification.

Above The raked gravel in the Abbot's Garden with its gracefully curved coastline is lent a seasonal touch by the weeping cherry tree. During the course of the year, the gravel is raked into different shapes, challenging viewers to find their own interpretation.

KOSHO-JI 興聖寺

An Atmospheric Soto Zen Monastery and Garden

FOUNDED 1233

Kosho-ji offers a rare chance in the Kyoto area to inspect a Soto Zen monastery. It is located in the small town of Uji, not far from the popular World Heritage site of Byodo-in. The riverside setting was a retreat for Heian aristocrats, who set up villas along the banks, and the final section of *Genji Monogatari* (c. 1006) takes place here. It is also known as 'the home of green tea', with a reputation for the high quality of its leaves. For those looking to combine history with small-town charm and Zen aesthetics, Kosho-ji makes an ideal outing.

The temple owes its origin to Eihei Dogen, founder of Soto Zen in Japan, and his life story is told in a set of pictures near the reception area. After studying with a Soto master in China, where he attained enlightenment, Dogen returned to Kennin-ji before going to live as a hermit in the Fukakusa area of Kyoto. From the disciples who gathered around his humble dwelling developed the temple of Kosho-ji. Dogen stayed for eleven years writing chapters of his masterwork, *Shobogenzo* (Treasury of the True Dharma Eye), before moving on to Fukui and Eihei-ji in 1244. After his departure, the Fukakusa temple was destroyed by fire, and it was not until the middle of

Left The temple's location dates back to 1648, when it was chosen by local ruler Nagai Naomasa. On the same river bank is Ujigami Jinja, which contains Japan's oldest surviving shrine structure, while on the opposite bank is another World Heritage Site, the Pure Land paradise of Byodo-in.
Opposite top The entrance gate, more squat than is usual in Japan, has a distinctly Chinese feel and is fashioned in the Sung style. It stands at the top of the Kotozaka Slope rising from the Uji River.
Opposite bottom "Until you feel, and keenly feel, that stones have character, that stones have tones and values," wrote Lafcadio Hearn, "the whole artistic meaning of a Japanese garden cannot be revealed to you."

the seventeenth century that it was reconstituted and relocated in Uji. The temple remains mindful of its important heritage, displaying the following notice:

In the present difficult situation of Japanese Buddhism, this temple endeavors to continue to be true to the essence of Dogen's interpretation of Zen, and to exist as a Buddhist temple rather than a tourist showpiece.

The approach to Kosho-ji, known as Kotosaka, leads up a slope from the Uji River, which is lined with maples and is spectacular in autumn. The entrance gate is in Chinese style, and within the grounds priests can be seen going about their business (there are twelve in all, with a handful of novices in training). Visitors are free to make their way unsupervised around the complex. There are a variety of gardens, the most attractive being a delightful pond garden contained

within the building complex. As the visitor approaches, the sound of flowing water can be heard, then all of a sudden the corridor opens up onto a carp pond fed by a small waterfall from the hillside behind.

The route passes around all the main buildings, including the hall for monks (Sodo), which is the oldest in the Soto sect. There are *zafu* meditation cushions in the corridor area for general use, but within the hall the tatami are reserved for specific monks.

A large wooden gong in the shape of a fish is hung from the rafters of Zen temples to be struck at meal times and for special events. Fish were thought to set a good example, since they never sleep but are always conscious.

KOSHO-JI AT A GLANCE

Founded 1233 by Eihei Dogen; 1648 refounded by the *daimyo* Nagai Naomasa. 'Temple of Promoting the Sacred'

Affiliation Eihei-ji School of Soto Zen

Special features Pond garden, Tenarai Kannon statue, blood-stained panels

Opening 9 am–5 pm (¥300)

Zazen 1st/3rd Sunday, 9–10 am (free). Trial meditation 30 mins, anytime 9 am–4.30 pm (¥500)

Event Oct, 1st Sunday, 10 am: new tea procession

Access 10 mins walk from Uji Station, Keihan line

Contact (0774) 21-2040

The Founder's Hall (Kaisando) has a revered statue of Dogen. One can also enter the Memorial Hall, where the names of prominent parishioners from the past are written on *ihai* (memorial tablets). The small room is dominated by a statue of Kannon, personification of compassion, whose big toe is raised in readiness to move when summoned.

In the Dharma Hall (Hatto), the gilded hangings before the Shakyamuni altar provide an ornate touch that contrasts with the spartan spareness of other rooms. Attention is drawn to the blood-stained ceiling (a handprint is circled in white), a ghoulish touch which derives from the Buddhist notion of pacifying tormented spirits. The wood originated in Fushimi Castle where a mass slaughter and suicide took place in 1600. The floorboards were subsequently dispersed among selected temples to soothe the souls of those who died.

Temple roofs have tiles made of fired clay. The oldest date back to the sixth century and were introduced from Korea. The end tiles usually bear *tomoe* swirls symbolizing water as a protective charm against fire.

Stone lanterns used in early Buddhism to illuminate paths were adopted by tea masters as decorative items. Different forms evolved, with the classic type comprising five distinct shapes to represent the five elements of Chinese cosmology.

Eihei Dogen (1200–1253)

Born into the nobility in Uji, Eihei Dogen lost both his parents at a young age, giving him a keen sense of life's fragility. At thirteen he stole away to Hiei, where he trained as a Tendai monk before leaving to study at Kennin-ji under Myozen, successor to the founder Myoan Eisai. In 1223, to further his understanding, Dogen went to study for four years in China, where he received Dharma transmission from the rigorous Rujing (Jp. Nyojo).

Upon his return to Japan, Dogen settled at Kennin-ji where he wrote a treatise about his understanding of *zazen* as 'just sitting'. It involves letting thoughts pass like clouds in the sky that come and go. His teaching encountered resistance from the traditionalists of Mt Hiei (at the time Kennin-ji was still nominally part of Tendai), so he moved out to a hermitage in Fukakusa in 1230, later receiving enough donations to set up an independent monastery named Kosho-ji. It was here that he started editing the first chapters of what was to become his life work, *Shobogenzo* (Treasury of the True Dharma Eye), a collection of lectures and commentaries comprising ninety-five chapters.

Because of the large number of disciples the charismatic Dogen attracted, the monks of Mt Hiei felt threatened and in 1243 tried to burn down Kosho-ji. It prompted him to move away, and with the backing of a feudal lord he was able to construct Eihei-ji in what is present-day Fukui Prefecture. Although he was later offered a temple in Kamakura by the shogun, he preferred the seclusion of Eihei-ji where he could preach and do his writing. When he was fifty-three he fell sick and traveled back to Kyoto for treatment, but passed away a month later.

Dogen wrote several works which outlined in methodical detail the techniques, rules and regulations by which a Soto community should be run. At the core of his thinking was the notion that meditation was not a means to an end but an end in itself. Those who have read the best-selling *Eat Sleep Sit* (2015) will know how zealously Dogen's teachings are followed, even after 800 years. For members of the Soto sect, he remains a personal guide in a very real sense.

Left The elegant rooflines of Tofuku-ji's enormous Sanmon gate. The only such gate not to be destroyed by fire, it is a National Treasure and houses statuary on the second floor (not usually accessible).

Opposite The east garden of the Founder's Hall is a dense composition of shrubs and rocks arranged on a slope, at the base of which is a pond with bridges. The result is a busy arrangement leading up to the lush vegetation beyond. By contrast, its counterpart on the western side is a flat dry landscape that takes its tone from the memorial building.

Below The Hasso Garden laid out by Mirei Shigemori around the Abbot's Quarters consists of four different dry landscapes. The western section has square-trimmed azalea bushes set amongst white gravel, in reference to the ancient Chinese style of rice fields. In this way, homage is paid to the overseas origins of Zen.

Bottom The thousands of trees in the Sengyokukan ravine draw packed crowds in late November when Tofuku-ji becomes synonymous with 'maple hunting'. The most prized spot is the Tsuten Bridge, from which there are stunning views to either side.

TOFUKU-JI 東福寺

A Maple Gorge and the Famous Shigemori Gardens

FOUNDED 1236

Tofuku-ji is one of the earliest Zen temples in Kyoto. It is also one of the most visually striking. Not only does it boast some of the largest Zen buildings in Japan but it has a dramatic gorge containing some 2,000 maples. Set against the backdrop of the Eastern Hills, the temple has an unusual sense of openness and no visible modern encroachment. The result is an appealing Zen atmosphere enhanced by discrete information boards in English. It is also a popular destination for garden lovers because of the celebrated modern creations. As well as the monastery, there are attractive subtemples and just twenty minutes walk away is the much-loved Shinto shrine of Fushimi Inari (now Kyoto's no. 1 tourist spot).

The temple was founded by a powerful aristocrat, who invited the influential Enni Ben'en (1202–80) to be the first abbot. It was an ambitious project, which aimed to recreate in

The northern section of the Hasso Garden tapers off as it extends towards azalea bushes, behind which maple trees rise out of the ravine beyond. The effect suggests progression towards emptiness and the unknown. Paul Klee and Wassily Kandinsky were among Shigemori's favorite artists and their influence is evident in the geometric design, although garden traditionalists objected to the grid pattern with its straight lines.

Kyoto the combined splendor of Nara's To(dai-ji) and (Ko)fuku-ji from a combination of which it derived its name. Construction took nineteen years to complete, but fire has ravaged the temple several times over the centuries, including most recently in 1881. As a result, though the buildings look ancient, they mostly date from the early twentieth century.

The layout is in classic style, with lotus pond, Sanmon gate, Lecture Hall (Hatto), and Abbot's Quarters (Hojo) aligned along a central axis facing south. The Imperial Messenger's Gate, unusually, faces west. The Sanmon is a formidable structure, the largest and oldest of any Zen gate in Japan. Built in 1425, it was painstakingly disassembled and repaired over nine years from 1969 to 1978. The second floor houses a sixteenth-century statue of the historical Buddha surrounded by *arhat* (enlightened beings), while the ceiling and pillars are covered in pictures of paradise.

To either side of the gate are recently restored toilets and bath house, which date from medieval times. The latrines, viewable through window openings, consist of regularly spaced circular holes and are nicknamed 'the 100 man toilets'. The baths used steam conveyed by duckboards into two wash rooms catering for up to 350 monks at a time. The steam softened the skin, enabling bodily dirt to be wiped off, and required far less consumption of wood and water than hot baths. "Even in

The white sand of the Hasso's South Garden is raked to suggest an ocean with whirlpools. Set within this are rock groupings which represent the islands of Horai, mythical paradise of Daoist Immortals. The conventional subject matter was chosen to match the formal face of the Abbot's Quarters, although the islands are given an unusually vigorous touch through their verticality.

those days people had a sense of ecology," notes the signboard.

To the north of the latrines stands the Zendo (Meditation Hall). The tiled gable roof surmounts a five-bay long ridge, making it the largest as well as the oldest Meditation Hall in the whole of Japan. It could hold up to 400 monks, who were each allotted one tatami mat on which to sleep, eat, study and practice. The Lecture Hall (Hatto or Hondo) was reconstructed in 1932 and an opening allows sight of the Shakyamuni image, flanked by attendants and protected by guardians. The dark interior also contains a Blue Dragon ceiling by Kyoto artist Insho Domoto (d. 1975). To commemorate the Buddha's death, a huge painting is displayed here each year which measures a staggering 7 x 14 meters.

Garden Sections

The northern half of the temple comprises two separate sections with an entrance fee. The Founder's Hall offers a chance to traverse the gorge

Enni Ben'en—The Father of Tofuku-ji (1202–1280)

Legends accrue around people of outstanding talents, and such was the case with Enni Ben'en. He was supposedly conceived when his mother saw Venus glittering in a dream (Buddha was enlightened when he saw Venus), and a priest predicted the child would become someone special. He began his training in Tendai Buddhism at the age of five, and later he studied under Myoan Eisai at Kennin-ji, where he had a vision of the deified Sugawara no Michizane, who told him to go to China. He remained there for six years studying under Wushuh Shinfan (known in Japan as Mujun) and receiving the Rinzai lineage.

On his return to Japan in 1241, Enni brought back noodle-making and water-power technology, which helped him in promoting Zen in northern Kyushu. Tradition claims he also brought the seeds with which the green tea of Shizuoka Prefecture originated. He acquired such a reputation that one of the leading members of the Fujiwara family, Kujo Michiie (1191–1252), invited him to Kyoto. This gave him a platform from which to introduce to the court the literature and culture of the Song Dynasty.

Enni's style of Zen embraced elements of Shingon and Tendai Buddhism, making it amenable to the aristocratic élite. He was known for his erudition and wisdom. In addition to his work at Tofuku-ji, he served as abbot of Kennin-ji and played a vital part in establishing Zen in Kyoto. Following his death, he was the first to be awarded the prestigious title of Kokushi (national priest). He left behind a short piece called *Zazen ron*, consisting of twenty-four questions and answers. His true legacy, though, and one for which his successors continue to honor his name, is the temple itself.

and view its historic gardens, while the Abbot's Hall is famous for the extraordinary modern gardens by Mirei Shigemori (1896–1975). Paying respects at the former before proceeding to the latter allows appreciation of just how cleverly Shigemori managed to be in applying a contemporary touch to the Japanese tradition.

The Founder's Hall is accessed either by a roofed bridge over the gorge or by following the path through the landscaped grounds. In the courtyard is a dry landscape on one side and an attractive pond garden on the other. These conventional Japanese gardens

prepare the visitor for the Abbot's Hall with its Hasso Garden, laid out by Shigemori on all four sides of the hall in 1939. It was so revolutionary that it is said to have propelled Zen into the modern age.

The main southern garden features four groups of rocks in raked gravel representing the Chinese Isles of the Immortals, as well as five mossy mounds symbolizing the 'mountain-temples' of the Gozan system (see page 14). The West Garden has square azalea bushes in the Chinese fashion, while in the North Garden is a checkered pattern of moss and square slabs which fades into a 'borrowed

landscape' of maple trees. The East Garden contains seven cylindrical pillars recycled from old foundation stones and positioned to symbolize the Big Dipper. From thoughts of the past, the garden leads the visitor to contemplation of the cosmos.

Subtemples

In Meiji times, Tofuku-ji was drastically reduced in size. Previously it used to have a hundred monks in residence, but at the time of writing there are just five. Once there were fifty-three subtemples but now there are only twenty-five. Most are closed to the public, but Sokushu-in and Ryogin-an,

At one end of the Hasso's South Garden are five mossy mounds representing the five 'mountains' (temples) of the Gozan system. In this innovative touch, Mirei Shigemori pays tribute to Tofuku-ji's role in the development of Zen.

TOFUKU-JI AT A GLANCE

Founded 1236 by Kujo Michiie, imperial chancellor; founding abbot Enni Ben'en. 'Temple of Eastern Happiness'

Affiliation Head of Tofuku-ji School of Rinzai Zen (25 subtemples, 367 branch temples)

Special features Sanmon gate, gorge with 2,000 maples, medieval baths and toilets, twentieth-century gardens

Opening 9 am–3.30 pm; Founder's Hall (¥400); Abbot's Hall (¥400)

Access Tofuku-ji Station, Nara or Keihan line, then 10 mins walk

Zazen Sundays 6.30–7.30 am in the Zendo (free)

Events March 14–16: Display of Nehan-zu for Buddha's anniversary, also special openings; Nov. 23: Fude Kuyo calligraphy at Shogaku-an

Contact (075) 561-0087 (http://www.tofukuji.jp/english/)

A checkerboard pattern in the western section of the Founder's Hall garden. The expanse of raked gravel is only interrupted by a compact grouping of bush, rock and tree in one corner, offsetting the flatness with height and color.

which are noted for their beautiful gardens, are open in November. Shogaku-an is known for calligraphy and on November 23 hosts a ceremony to pacify the spirits of old writing brushes. Myoan-ji, long associated with the *shakuhachi* flute (see page 34), is usually closed but acts as head of the once flourishing Fuke Sect.

One other subtemple of note is Shorin-ji, which was built in 1550 and houses a Bishamonten statue (guardian of the north). Normally closed, it offers several options on a reservation basis only: introduction to *zazen* (¥1000); *shakyo* (copying sutras) and *shabutsu* (copying Buddhist images), ¥1500 each including a green tea set. There are occasional sessions in healing Zen, or Zen and yoga, and opportunity for *shojin ryori* temple meals. See the website, or email in English to shorinjitemple@gmail.com.

The eastern section of the Hasso Garden features seven pillars in the form of the Big Dipper. The constellation was a prominent feature of East Asian cosmology and in Daoism it was thought to control people's destiny. On another level, the dipper is used at religious sites as a means of purification. By its use of recycled pillars (Zen believes nothing should go to waste), the garden is invested with historical as well as spiritual significance.

Funda-in (Sesshu-ji)

芬陀院

A Classic Garden Reborn

FOUNDED 1321

This Crane and Tortoise Garden is thought to have originated with fifteenth-century artist Sesshu Toyo. It was for long neglected and was even used to grow sweet potatoes. In 1939, garden designer Mirei Shigemori was invited to reconstruct it, and he added a section on the eastern side.

Officially called Funda-in, this subtemple is more widely known as Sesshu-ji for its connection with Japan's 'genius of black ink', Sesshu Toyo (1420–1506). A one-time monk at Shokoku-ji, he stayed at this subtemple later in life on his visits to Kyoto and landscaped the garden. By 1939 it had long fallen into disrepair, and Mirei Shigemori (1896–1975), designer of the Hasso Garden at Tofuku-ji, was asked to remodel it.

In the main section, Shigemori largely kept to the original composition, which features a Horai garden of white sand in the foreground. Beyond it lies a moss garden with two rock groupings to represent the felicitous Crane and Turtle Islands. The Crane Island has taller rocks, the Turtle Island is lower and has a double level of stones with a protuberance for the head. The overall effect is of an enclosed 'paradise', with bamboo peering over the top of trees on all three sides and the only sound the chirping of birds.

In the adjoining eastern section, Shigemori added a series of stones embedded in moss, which according to the temple leaflet may represent the Four Islands of the Immortals. It is best viewed from the wooden veranda that runs round the Main Hall and leads to the Tonantei tea house with its circular window. In Buddhism, the circle represents the totality of the universe, but it can also represent perfection, and the sublime view here could indeed be called a perfect universe.

The temple boasts one or two artistic touches in keeping with its heritage, for instance, dried leaf inserts in its paper *shoji* screens, and a delightful flower arrangement in the water flowing through a stone wash basin. A green tea set is available on the veranda for those wishing to sit and ponder the combined genius of Sesshu and Shigemori, two creative artists 500 years apart but joined in the vision of Horai, an ideal world free of aging and suffering.

FUNDA-IN AT A GLANCE

Founded 1321 by Ichijo Tsunemichi; founding priest Sozen Jozan. 'Subtemple of the White Lotus'

Affiliation Tofuku-ji School of Rinzai Zen

Special features Mirei Shigemori remodeled garden

Opening 9 am–4.30 pm (¥300); green tea set (¥600)

Access 5 mins walk from Tofuku-ji Station, JR or Keihan line

Contact (075) 541-1761

REIUN-IN 霊雲院

A Celebrated Modern Rock Garden

FOUNDED 1390

In the middle of the swirling sea created by Mirei Shigemori is a plinth bearing a 'relic stone' gifted to the temple in times past. The structure represents Mt Meru, or Sumeru, at the center of Buddhist cosmology. According to tradition, the mythical mountain is shaped like an hourglass with a square base and a narrow middle.

Deeply raked gravel circles a plinth surmounted by a curiously shaped rock. Dynamic swirls suggest whirlpools. In the background are moss-covered mounds and a 'dry stream' feeding the swirling 'ocean'. The garden is named Nine Mountains Eight Seas, which refers to the ancient Indian view of the cosmos. The suggestion here is that the swirling seas center around Mt Sumeru, mythical mountain at the heart of the Buddhist universe. It is quite unlike anything the visitor will have seen before, and the overall effect is of irresistible forces at work.

The garden was originally laid out in the sixteenth century but had fallen into disrepair when, in 1970, Mirei Shigemori was asked to recreate it. In a visionary move, he made the focal point a 'relic stone' which had been gifted to the temple by the seventeenth-century feudal lord Hosokawa Tadatoshi. The unusually shaped rock thus acts as a miniaturized symbol of cosmic proportions.

The main room has specially large windows for viewing the garden, with its juxtaposition of modern and traditional. The 'dry river' flows into a separate section along the western side of the building, which contains a landscape named 'Bowing Clouds'. Again, it is daringly unconventional, with an irregular section of strikingly brown sand along the side of the building. Is it a shoreline, or does it represent clouds? It is up to the viewer, says the temple.

Although the whole focus of the subtemple is on the Shigemori garden, there are some other items of interest, including the altar with its Zen trappings. The nearby *tokonoma* alcove has a fine hanging scroll of Daruma, while the back window looks out onto an unusual two-storey tea room from the Momoyama period. The ground floor overlooks the Bowing Clouds Garden, while the second floor floats serenely 'above the clouds'. The simple use of water basin, stone lanterns and moss transform what would otherwise be a bland enclosure into a quintessentially Japanese scene. In its own modest way, it is as illustrative of Zen aesthetics as the celebrated garden opposite.

REIUN-IN AT A GLANCE

Foundation 1390 by the Zen monk Kiyo Hoshu. 'Subtemple of the Auspicious Cloud'
Affiliation Tofuku-ji School of Rinzai Zen
Special features Gardens by Mirei Shigemori
Opening hours 9 am–4 pm but irregular; best to check first (¥300)
Access A few mins walk from Tofukuji Station, JR or Keihan line
Contact (075) 561-4080

KOMYO-IN 光明院
A Haven of Quietude
FOUNDED 1391

Above The circular window in Zen has spiritual as well as aesthetic significance, for the full moon symbolizes completion of the lunar cycle and hence enlightenment. The shape also recalls the round mirror of Buddhist altars, which sets an example to worshippers of ego-less reflection.
Below One characteristic of a Shigemori garden is the placement of rocks. Shape, size, spacing and the lay of the land are vital considerations. Vantage points thus play a vital part as they present the positioning in the way the designer intended.

Almost uniquely, Komyo-in has managed to retain charming, old-fashioned ways. Even in these commercial times, the temple simply puts out a bamboo pole into which people are asked to put 'donations'. The reception is unmanned, the doors are wide open and visitors are welcome to wander round at their leisure. For those in want of quiet reflection after a visit to Tofuku-ji, this is the place to take time out. It is one of the last oases of calm open to the public.

There are tatami rooms and an altar room to explore, but the main feature is the garden by acclaimed designer Mirei Shigemori (1896–1975). There are three viewing spots, each offering a different perspective: from the tea room, the study room and the Main Hall. The latter provides a picture-frame view through its open sliding doors onto a scene that is designed to change with the seasons (the garden has cherry blossom, azalea bushes and maple trees).

The garden contains raked gravel and mossy mounds, punctuated by a profusion of standing stones (characteristic of Shigmori). There are three different groupings of vertical rocks, which represent three different Buddhist triads. These lend the composition a firm triangular base. Other rocks are positioned like rays spreading out from the large central altar stone, similar to the rays emanating from Buddha referenced in the temple's name. There is also a suggestion of lunar illumination in the name of the garden, Hashin

The Main Hall with surrounding veranda offers different perspectives of Mirei Shigemori's garden. The three rocks on the rise to the right signify the historical Buddha and his attendants, Fugen and Monju. There are two other triads in the garden, which lend a strong sense of presence, with other rocks spilling outwards like rays of illumination.

no niwa (Garden of the Wave-Mind), as referenced in Zen poetry.

> **Over the mountain peak**
> **No clouds appear,**
> **The moon among the waves**

In Buddhism, the moon is a symbol of clarity and understanding.

The moon theme is taken up in a round window with bamboo lattice-work (not the one pictured opposite). It exemplifies *wabi-sabi*: simple, natural, made with perishable materials and aesthetically pleasing. The circle is a Buddhist symbol of enlightenment and the asymmetrical arrangement of sticks a dynamic channeling of energy. The effect is to heighten awareness of being apart from, yet a part of, the outside world, for the lattice is a barrier-less barrier in an open window through which air flows freely. As the scene is internalized by the viewer, within and without merge into one. The aesthetics are thus more than a matter of beauty but a powerful lesson in the Zen way of thinking.

KOMYO-IN AT A GLANCE

Founded 1391 by Kinzan Myosho. 'Subtemple of Illumination'

Affiliation Tofuku-ji School of Rinzai Zen

Special features Mirei Shigemori garden

Opening 8 am to sunset (¥300)

Access 2 mins walk further south from the south gate of Tofuku-ji

Contact (075) 561-7317

NANZEN-JI 南禅寺

Kyoto's Most Prestigious Zen Monastery

FOUNDED 1291

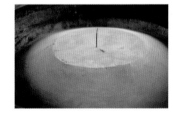

Nanzen-ji has been called 'the world's most important Zen temple' because in the past it stood alone at the top of the Gozan system of patronage (a signboard at the entrance proudly proclaims the status). The temple has a long list of notable abbots, and with its close connections to the ruling class it was able to acquire priceless assets. The prestige it enjoyed was echoed in its size, for at one time there were sixty-two subtemples and over a thousand monks. Now, following the

cuts of Meiji times there are thirteen subtemples and, at the time of writing, just six monks in training. Although it may be only a fraction of what it once was, there remains much to see in terms of art and architecture.

The temple owes its foundation to an exorcism. Emperor Kameyama, who abdicated at twenty-six to escape the shackles of the shogunate, built a retirement villa in the eastern hills, which turned out to be haunted. He called in leading monks to exorcise the

ghost and after several failures turned to the abbot of Tofuku-ji, Mukan Fumon, who was able to settle the problem by a lengthy period of *zazen* sitting meditation with his followers. Impressed, Kameyama determined to turn part of his palace into a Zen temple, with Fumon as the founding abbot. He also took orders as a priest; thus the religion of the samurai had taken root within the imperial family.

The temple was destroyed on three different occasions during Muromachi times, but it was rebuilt in even grander style during the late sixteenth and seventeenth centuries. Unusually, it is aligned towards the west so as to back onto the Higashiyama hills. The openness of the precincts, together with an aqueduct added in Meiji times, gives the temple a different feel from the walled communities elsewhere.

The Abbot's Quarters

The grounds are dominated by a magnificent Sanmon gate, one of the three largest in Japan, and climbing the steep staircase enables a close-up view of the formidable woodwork involved. From the second floor is an expansive view over the city, which for the Japanese is invariably linked with a Kabuki play featuring the robber Ishikawa Goemon. "Zekkei kana!" (What a great scene!), he was famously moved to say. In the altar room is a painted ceiling of phoenixes attributed to master artist Kano Tanyu (1602–74), and among the statuary is the shogun

Tokugawa Ieyasu and his general Todo Takatora, benefactor of the gate.

On the way to the Abbot's Quarters, it is worth peering into the gloomy interior of the Lecture Hall (Hatto) through the opening for worshippers. Inside is the main object of worship, Shakyamuni, flanked by two bodhi-sattva, Monju and Fugen. The ceiling is supported by massive zelkova pillars, and from out of the darkness looms a Sacred Dragon painted in 1909 by Kyoto artist Imao Keinen.

The extensive Abbot's Quarters house a small treasure trove of Japanese art. The buildings are divided into Small (Sho-hojo) and Large Quarters (Dai-hojo), and between them they reflect the prestige the temple once enjoyed. The former were once part of Hideyoshi's Fushimi Castle, while the Large Quarters were moved from the Imperial Palace. (It explains why this building is shingled, whereas Buddhist roofs are usually tiled.) There are over a hundred

Above The subtemple of Tenju-an, as seen from the Sanmon gate. In Mishima's *The Temple of the Golden Pavilion*, a woman is seen here giving her lover tea to which she adds her breast milk.
Below A monk crosses the temple precincts in short socks and open sandals. Learning to adjust to the bitter cold of winter is part of the training in austerity.

paintings in all, with nature scenes and Chinese figures at the forefront. Some of the most eye-catching are by celebrated artists of Momoyama times, when bold compositions expressed the optimistic mood of a newly unified nation. Replica panels recreate the originals with a brightness that is almost shocking in intensity.

There are several gardens, the most famous of which is a dry landscape laid out by master designer Kobori Enshu around 1600. It is named *Young Tigers Crossing the Water* in reference to the rock shapes (though this requires a stretch of the imagination). The tiger theme is picked up in sliding screen paintings by Kano Tanyu, amongst which the *Water-Drinking Tiger* has won special attention for its powerful yin–yang combination. The power and strength of the tiger (yang) is balanced by water or slender bamboo (yin), and the subtle lighting in the dark room makes the gold leaf background glow as if the sun is illuminating the forest.

For those who wish to take this all in afterwards, there is a tatami room at

The Lecture Hall, or Hatto, is not open to the public but through an opening one can peep inside at the statue of Shakyamuni and his two attendants. On the ceiling is a dragon painted by the early twentieth-century artist Keinen Imao.

the exit where visitors can enjoy a green tea set while gazing therapeutically at a small waterfall (¥500 at reception). It offers occasion, too, to reflect on the words of former abbot Sotetsu Katsuhira (d. 1983):

The Zen path is not concerned with distinguishing good from bad, love from hate, beauty from ugliness. Rather, at its heart lies the perpetual equality of all things to which we can open our eyes and hearts.... If we allow ourselves to live with our hearts open to the world, we can live each day as if it is the finest.

Surrounds

In Meiji times, Nanzen-ji was saddled with a brick-built aqueduct, which carried water from Lake Biwa, seven miles to the east. It was part of a massive undertaking and one of the first examples of western technology in the fast modernizing country. The canal from Lake Biwa finished next to Nanzen-ji, where a sudden drop necessitated an incline with rail track (popular in cherry blossom time). It prompted the construction of Japan's first power station (1891). Ironically, the Western-inspired aqueduct has weathered so well into its Zen surroundings that it is now a popular item with photographers.

Although the temple is thronged at peak seasons, particularly maple-viewing time, it remains a functioning monastery and the handful of monks may occasionally be seen working in the grounds. The area is famous for its tofu restaurants, since the protein-laden food, easy on the digestion, was an important part of the monastical diet. Restaurants such as Junsei, Taian-en and Okutan provide a traditional Japanese atmosphere in which to savor the food.

Because Nanzen-ji is nestled against the Eastern Hills, there are attractive trails from the temple into the surrounding nature. A ten-minute walk skirting the eastern cemetery takes one to a site of ancient asceticism, with statuary and waterfall. Or walk along the aqueduct and bear left uphill to the sun-worshipping Himukai Shrine. Alternatively, there are magical experiences to be had in the off-hours, such as visiting Nanzen-ji in the evening when the massive buildings loom large in the shadows. Or get up at dawn to enjoy the lichen-encrusted maples glistening in the early morning sunlight and be the very first visitor of the day to mount the steps of the Sanmon. At such moments, like the robber Ishikawa Goemon, you too may be moved to exclaim "Zekkei kana!"

NANZEN-JI AT A GLANCE

Founded 1291 by Emperor Kameyama; founding priest Mukan Fumon (abbot of Tofuku-ji). 'Temple of the Southern School of Zen'

Affiliation Head of the Nanzen-ji School of Rinzai (13 subtemples, 427 branch temples)

Special features Gardens and artwork, Sanmon gate, aqueduct and surrounds

Opening 8.40 am–5 pm; 4.30 pm Dec–Feb; grounds (free); Sanmon gate (¥500); Abbot's Quarters (¥500; tea ¥500)

Event Apr 8: Hanamatsuri for Buddha's birthday; Dec 31: Ringing of New Year bell (apply in advance for a number)

Access 5 mins from Keage Station, Tozai line

Zazen 2nd/4th Sun in Ryoen-kaku (free); Apr–Oct 6–7 am, Nov–Mar 6.30–7.30 am

Contact (075) 771-0365 (zen.rinnou.net)

NANZEN-IN 南禅院
An Elegant Hillside Pond Garden
FOUNDED 1291

Nanzen-in stands on the original site of Emperor Kameyama's retirement villa, and it was from this small temple that the larger monastery took its name. It is reached by passing under the incongruous brick aqueduct of Meiji times, and its location at the foot of the Eastern Hills remains key to an appreciation of the garden which merges into the surrounding hillside.

The main building is an elegant structure, donated in 1703 by the devout mother of the fifth Tokugawa shogun, Tsunayoshi. The roof is considered a masterpiece of *kokera-buki*—layers of small cypress shingles fixed with wooden nails. Inside are black ink *fusuma* paintings by the Kano School and an altar statue of the founder, Emperor Kameyama.

The original garden was destroyed in the Onin War (1467–77), after which it underwent alterations. It is said that the choicest items of the day were assembled for its creation: cherry trees were brought from Yoshino, maples from Tatsuta, reeds from Namba and even frogs from Ide. The layout centers around the Sogenchi Pond of two parts fed by a waterfall and surrounded by cedars and delicate maples. The water is shallow to reflect the deep greens of the woods. The lower pond is formed like the Chinese character for *kokoro* (heart-mind),

whereas the upper pond is supposedly shaped like a dragon and contains a representation of the Horai Isles of the Blessed.

In the northeast corner stands a mausoleum containing a portion of the ashes of Emperor Kameyama. From this vantage point, one supposes, his spirit must gaze with satisfaction over the garden and his wider legacy. Out of the converted wing of his retirement palace arose a place of contemplation that for centuries has fostered the deep communion of humans with nature.

NANZEN-IN AT A GLANCE

Founded 1291 by retired Emperor Kameyama. 'Subtemple of Southern School of Zen'

Affiliation Nanzen-ji School of Rinzai Zen

Special features Stroll garden

Opening 8.30 am–5 pm (¥300)

Access 1 min from Nanzen-ji main building; 5 mins from Keage Station, Tozai line

Contact 075 771-0365

Above The subtemple features a masterpiece of *kokera-buki* roofing, made up of layers of small cypress shingles.
Below The Sogenchi Pond, shaped as the Chinese character for *kokoro*, forms 'the heart' of the garden. In the shallow water is reflected the hillside greenery so as to double the effect of seasonal change.

TENJU-AN 天授庵

Breathtaking Maple Colors and Ponds

FOUNDED 1336

The fourteenth-century stroll garden was remodeled in 1605 and modified in the late nineteenth century. The pond has two sections divided by peninsulas to which a waterfall provides a pleasant backdrop. In late November, illumination of the autumn colors creates stunning lighting effects.

Imagine dazzling autumn colors reflected in ponds, framed by a wooden opening. You sit on the edge of a tatami room, taking in the view and enjoying the gentle breeze. Greens and browns merge into deep reds, and in the shadows murky figures move in the gathering gloom. In a city of marvels, the view of changing maple leaves through the open doors of Tenju-an must count among the most magical.

The Hermitage was built to honor the memory of Mukan Fumon, the founding priest of Nanzen-ji, and a life-size statue of him stands in the main building. The stroll garden was added in the late fourteenth century, and peninsulas extending from opposite sides divide its pond into two sections with varied shorelines. Later remodeling altered the original composition, one example being a bridge added in Meiji times to connect an island in the western pool to the 'mainland'.

The subtemple was destroyed by fire in 1447, and then again in the Onin War (1467–77). The present buildings date from 1602 and were financed by the *daimyo* Hosokawa Yusai, who is buried in the cemetery. The Main Hall (Hondo) faces east onto a dry landscape garden, in front of which a geometric pathway of rectangular stones set in white sand leads to the Main Gate, which is only used for ceremonial purposes.

On the sliding doors of the Main Hall are thirty-two black ink paintings executed in the early seventeenth century by Hasegawa Tohaku when he was sixty-four. As well as cranes and pine trees the pictures depict Zen teaching. One shows Chinese master Joshu, with shoes on his head in reference to a *koan* (Zen riddle) about non-duality. Such pictures are intended to provoke a different mode of perception. With a dry landscape in the east and a pond garden to the south, Tenju-an offers the visitor ample opportunity to sit and contemplate their enigmatic nature.

Above The temple's east garden features a formal path leading from an entrance gate that is never opened except for imperial visits. The decorative border, rigid right angle, and the restraint of the raking show high respect for the intended guest, with the lush greenery kept at a respectful distance.
Below The path to the pond garden shows greater informality with its gentle curve and irregular stones. It passes through a symbolic *chumon* gate, marking a division between the public outer garden and the more intimate inner garden.

TENJU-AN AT A GLANCE

Founded 1336 by the Nanzen-ji abbot Kokan Shiren; patron Emperor
    Kogon. 'Hermitage of the Heavenly Gift'
Affiliation Nanzen-ji School of Rinzai Zen
Special features Pond garden, dry landscape garden, artwork
Opening 9 am–5 pm
Event Nov 15–early Dec: illumination
Access 5 mins from Keage Station, Tozai line
Contact (075) 771-0744

KONCHI-IN 金地院
A Compact Garden Tour
FOUNDED C.1400

Konchi-in packs a lot into a compact space. There is a Chinese-style entrance gate, an acclaimed stroll garden, a Shinto shrine and a Main Hall with superb Momoyama-era paintings. The buildings date from 1605 when the temple was restored by Nanzen-ji's powerful abbot-statesman Ishin Suden (1569–1633). Like Thomas Wolsey, he combined his religious role with high politics, being close advisor to the first three Tokugawa shoguns and helping shape foreign policy. Recently, the subtemple has reached out to foreigners with English-language information, and wifi is available in front of the Hojo(!). Nonetheless, it remains a favorite of Kyoto lovers through being a microcosm of Japanese arts.

The garden was laid out by the leading designer of the time, Kobori Enshu, in expectation of a shogunal visit (which never took place). It is the temple's showpiece, but after being offered a glimpse, the visitor is led away by the path, around a pond and up a moss-lined slope. Only after heading back down again, and paying respects at the Founder's Hall, does one arrive at the main building from where the garden can be properly viewed. (In Japanese aesthetics, one approaches the main feature tangentially rather than directly.)

It comes as a surprise to find at the top of the slope a Shinto shrine deifying the shogun Tokugawa Ieyasu. Built in 1628, it was part of a national cult promoted by Ieyasu's grandson to strengthen the authority of the dynasty. Unusually, the building has a Buddhist

Left Stepping stones lead towards the Tosho-gu shrine, built in 1628 to honour the first Tokugawa shogun, Ieyasu.
Left below The Horai Garden (1632) has a Turtle Island (for longevity) on the left. In the middle is a Buddhist triad, before which lies a long altar stone for worship of Ieyasu's spirit in the Tosho-gu shrine shielded by the trees. To the right, a Crane Island (prosperity) is surmounted by a red pine, while the backdrop of undulating bushes, suggestive of rising hills, leads the eye up towards the 'borrowed scenery' of Higashiyama.
Right The garden path leads away from the temple's main buildings and up an adjoining slope. Only after touring the grounds is the visitor brought to the veranda of the main hall, from which the composition pictured below left can be viewed at leisure.
Bottom Stepping stones embedded in moss at the Benten Pond lead to a small shrine for the Goddess of Arts and Creativity. It is an example of Zen's syncretism with Shinto.

front to which a Shinto sanctuary is attached, making for a rare architectural hybrid. It is one of two Shinto shrines in the precincts, this being ancestral and the other animist, illustrative of the importance Zen attaches both to the bond with nature and to the national identity.

From the Abbot's Quarters (Hojo) is a panoramic view of the Horai Garden. Beautiful in itself, the rising layers and trimmed bushes merge into the contours of the Eastern Hills. In the foreground, a sea of raked gravel laps against a Turtle Island (to the left) and a Crane Island (to the right), symbols of a happy and long life. Between them lies a long flat 'altar stone', as if in worship of nature. The central rocks, which symbolize Mt Horai and the Isles of the Blessed, can by inference be taken to embrace the unseen presence of Ieyasu.

Within the Abbot's Quarters are early Edo paintings by leading members of the Kano School. For most people that is special enough, but the temple has more precious items that are held back for special tours (by reservation). These include an eight-windowed tea house by Kobori Enshu and a famous painting by Hasegawa Tohaku of a monkey reaching for the reflection of the moon in a pond—a Buddhist parable about the pursuit of illusion. Ironically, in a temple of treasures the most cherished item speaks of non-attachment.

KONCHI-IN AT A GLANCE

Founded c. 1400 by shogun Ashikaga Yoshimochi; founding priest Daigo Tokuki Zenshi; restored 1605 by Ishin Suden. 'Subtemple of the Golden Ground'

Affiliation Nanzen-ji School of Rinzai Zen

Special features Garden and tea house, artwork, Tosho-gu mausoleum

Opening 8.30 am–5 pm; 4.30 pm Dec–Feb (¥400). Special tour hourly from 9.30 except 12.30 (¥700). English language brochure (¥100)

Access 5 mins walk from Keage Station, Tozai line

Contact (075) 771-3511

DAITOKU-JI 大徳寺

Dry Landscapes and 'The Home of the Tea Ceremony'

FOUNDED 1325

Within the walled compound of Daitoku-ji is one of Kyoto's largest and most influential temples. For garden lovers, history buffs and practitioners of tea, it is a much prized destination. Shielded by walls from the surrounding roads, it exudes a surprising sense of calm. For much of its 700-year-old history the temple developed outside the Gozan system (see page 14) and experienced changing fortunes.

Founded by a retired emperor, it enjoyed imperial backing, but after being destroyed in the fifteenth century it was restored by the trading merchants of Sakai. Thereafter it found favor with samurai, as Japan's feuding warlords donated funds for subtemples (in effect family memorials). Later, in the nineteenth century, the temple was badly hit by the anti-Buddhist movement of Meiji times, being

reduced in size by two-thirds. Once it had had over sixty subtemples but now there are just twenty-two.

The temple originated in the encounter between retired Emperor Hanazono and the Zen monk Shuho Myocho. The latter had built a small hermitage in the north of Kyoto in 1315, but had subsequently gone to live with the beggars under Gojo Bridge. When the cloistered Emperor Hanazono heard of this, he went to the bridge and told the beggars that whoever could get a delicious melon without using their feet could have it. "Then give it to me without using your arms," retorted one of the throng. It was enough for Hanazono to recognize the master, and the encounter led to friendship between the two men.

In 1325, the former emperor turned Myocho's hermitage into a temple, which soon became no. 1 in the Gozan system. As is standard in Zen monasteries, the main buildings are aligned along a north–south axis. The Chakushimon is a gilded Chinese-style

The bell-shaped windows introduced from China are known as *katamado*. This example at Kohrin-in typifies the early style, with almost sheer vertical sides. Over time, the shape was refined, with graceful curves being added for aesthetic reasons.

Above Ikkyu Sojun (1394–1481), Japan's much loved rascal monk.
Left The formal pathway leading to the Abbot's Quarters. Unlike the subtemples with their lush approaches, the Chinese-style buildings at the core of the monastery have austere surrounds with wide avenues of gravel and occasional trees.
Right Flower decorations serve as a reminder of nature's bounty. Stone, bamboo and moss typify the traditional aesthetics of simplicity, harmony and natural beauty.

gate, relocated from the Imperial Palace, and the Sanmon gate was painted vermilion in Momoyama times. To its north stands the Buddha Hall, the doors of which are left open for worshippers, and from out of the darkness gleams the gilded image of Shakyamuni. Beyond that stand the Abbot's Quarters, open to the public in November, with *fusuma* pictures by master artist Kano Tanyu (1602–74), who also painted the Cloud Dragon on the ceiling in the Lecture Hall (Hatto).

Famous Figures

Daitoku-ji has been associated with many famous figures over its long history, not the least of whom was 'the wild man of Zen', Ikkyu Sojun (1394–1481). Rebel, poet and iconoclast, he was a man of many talents with a circle of influential followers. When the temple was destroyed in 1468 in the Onin War, Ikkyu was pressed to be abbot although by nature he had a strong

anti-authoritarian streak. Such was his respect for founder Shuho Myocho, however, that he accepted the task, and thanks to his connections with the wealthy merchants of Sakai the temple was restored (see page 126).

A later figure associated with Daitoku-ji was the martial arts guru Takuan Soho (1573–1643). He came to study at the temple aged fourteen, and at the unusually young age of thirty-six was appointed abbot, although he soon left to raise funds. An adviser to the top swordsmen of the time, Yagyu Munenori and Miyamoto Musashi, Takuan developed the concept of *mushin* (no-mind), in which complete

awareness is unadulterated by focus on any particular point.

Most of the formative tea masters in Japanese history were also associated with Daitoku-ji. Indeed, the temple is known as 'the face of tea', for it was here that the tea ceremony took shape. Outstanding figures include Ikkyu's disciple Murata Juko (1423–1502) as well as Sen no Rikyu (1522–91), Sen Sotan (1578–1658) and Kobori Enshu (1579–1647). Of these, Sen no Rikyu is the most important as he set the standards that still prevail today (see page 83).

In recent times, Daitoku-ji hosted an important group of Westerners centered around Ruth Fuller Sasaki, an American who played a vital role in the furthering of Zen in the West. She was the first ever foreigner and the first

Daitoku-ji lies within a world of walls, separating the sacred from the profane and the private from the public. The mud walls topped with tiles have won interest in recent years for their low environmental impact.

SHUHO MYOCHO (1282–1337)

Shuho Myocho, founder of Daitoku-ji, was given the posthumous title of Daito Kokushi, which translates as National Teacher of the Great Lamp.

Born in Hyogo, Shuho Myocho studied Tendai Buddhism as a youth but came to feel that knowledge of the scriptures was insufficient. He turned instead to Zen with its emphasis on practice. He was a disciple of Koho Kenichi, the teacher of Muso Soseki (1275–1351), and after becoming a priest he achieved enlightenment and spent time in Kamakura, where he was briefly abbot of Kencho-ji. He subsequently returned to Kyoto, spending over seven years living with beggars under Gojo Bridge.

> Sitting in meditation
> one sees people
> crossing and re-crossing the bridge
> just as they are. (tr. Richard Bryan McDaniel)

As founding abbot of Daitoku-ji, he modeled the institution on the rigorous lines set in China. Known for his strictness, he was zealous in practice and spoke out against attachment to material things. He could be direct, too: at a grand debate with priests from other sects, an opponent held out a box in which he claimed the whole universe was contained. Daito's response was immediate: he smashed it to pieces.

The teaching at Daitoku-ji emphasized *kensho* (awakening), and students were urged to consider "the original countenance that they had before they were born". Daito put little stock in those who simply followed the rules. "On the other hand, if you carry on your activities with the eye of *kensho*, though you pass your days living in a solitary hut in the idleness, wear a battered robe, and eat only boiled roots, you are the man who meets me face to face every day."

The most famous story about Daito concerns his lameness. He had always emphasized correctness of posture in *zazen*, so he was frustrated in later life by not being able to bend his leg. Determined to force it into the correct position, he broke a bone and caused blood to flow down his robe, but in a legendary display of resoluteness he mastered the pain and remained sitting calmly. It is one of several examples of dedication that, 700 years later, still serves to motivate those who follow in his path.

ever female to head a Zen subtemple (Ryosen-an). Amongst those employed in her research team was the poet Gary Snyder as well as the scholars Philip Yampolsky and Burton Watson.

Tea Matters

Daitoku-ji boasts thirty tea houses in all, some of which are highly valued National Treasures only accessible by tea groups or during special openings. Some of the most prized have ties to Sen no Rikyu, master of masters, particularly those at the Juko-in subtemple (which houses his grave) and also Daisen-in, where the supremo Toyotomi Hideyoshi went to study with him.

The son of a Sakai merchant, Sen no Rikyu, took an interest in tea from a young age, and his lessons were accompanied by training at Daitoku-ji.

By middle age he had acquired such a reputation that he was appointed tea master to the unifiers of Japan, Oda Nobunaga and Toyotomi Hideyoshi.

DAITOKU-JI AT A GLANCE

Founded 1325 by retired Emperor Hanazono; founding priest Shuho Myocho (Daito Kokushi). 'Temple of Great Virtue'

Affiliation Head of Daitoku-ji School of Rinzai Zen (22 subtemples, 201 branch temples)

Special features Dry landscape gardens, four subtemples open to the public, Izusen *shojin ryori* restaurant (¥3500 and up)

Opening Grounds (free); subtemples 9 am–4.30 pm

Zazen At Ryosen-an, 7–8 am; irregular, ring first (075) 491-0543 (donation)

Events Spring and autumn (irregular): special opening of main buildings; Oct 2nd Sun: Bakuryo-ten airing in Hatto

Access Kitaoji subway station, 15 mins walk. Bus 101, 205, 206 to Daitokuji-mae

Contact (075) 491-0019 (zen.rinnou.net)

Despite worldly advancement, Rikyu remained concerned with the spiritual aspect of the ceremony: "Though you wipe your hands and brush off the dust and dirt from the vessels, what is the use of all this fuss if the heart is still impure?"

In terms of tea, the temple's Sanmon gate is of particular note. It is a striking structure, not only for its unusual coloring but because a second floor and external stairways have been added to the original single storey. As benefactor, Rikyu had a statue of himself installed among the second-floor images, as was customary. This apparently outraged Hideyoshi, for on his visits to study tea he would pass beneath the gate, meaning that symbolically Rikyu was in a 'superior' position. In 1591, out of the blue, Hideyoshi vengefully ordered his tea master to commit ritual suicide. For restoring the Sanmon gate, Sen no Rikyu paid with his life.

As 'the home of tea', Daitoku-ji contains appealing *roji* (dewy paths), which lead in many cases to celebrated tea houses. Some are valuable in their own right and some have great historical significance, such as those used by tea master Sen no Rikyu.

Detail of the A-Un Garden, which features two complementary rocks. A-Un refers to the unity of opposites, such as inhalation and exhalation which combine to form one breath.

RYOGEN-IN 龍源院

A Classic Set of Abbot's Quarters

FOUNDED 1502

This subtemple provides a perfect opportunity to study the classic layout of an Abbot's Quarters, since each of the six rooms has an explanatory notice in English describing its use: reception, altar, patrons' room, study, storage and living area. The building was erected in 1502 and is the oldest of its type in Japan. It contains precious Chinese ink paintings, and the object of worship is a statue of Shakyamuni dating back to 1250. Together with the Main Hall, it can boast a total of five small gardens.

The southern set of rooms, where eminent guests were received, look onto a formal Horai garden with a sea of raked white sand containing rock formations symbolizing Turtle and Crane Islands. In the far corner, upright rocks represent the fount of life emerging from the Blessed Isles of the Immortals. (Interestingly, the garden only took its present form after a 700-year-old tree withered and died in 1980.)

The garden to the north, attributed to master designer Soami (d. 1525), consists of a moss garden with a large standing rock. It is the oldest garden in Daitoku-ji and illustrates Buddhist cosmology, in which oceans flow around Mt Sumeru at the center of the universe. It would have served as a means of instruction for the abbot's students. "This is the absolute

RYOGEN-IN AT A GLANCE

Founded 1502 by the lord of Noto with the Daitoku-ji priest Tokei Soboku. (The temple's name refers to the Chinese teacher Shogen Sugaku). 'Subtemple of the Dragon Master' (Shogen Sugaku)

Affiliation Daitoku-ji School of Rinzai Zen

Special features Dry landscape, rock and moss gardens, oldest Zen-style building

Opening 9 am–4.30 pm (¥350)

Access Bus 206 to Daitokuji-mae, then 3 mins walk

Contact (075) 491-7635

humanity that we all innately possess, the original form which no one can violate," notes the temple leaflet. "Discovering this on one's own is Zen enlightenment."

In the Main Hall are historical items, such as a Tanegashima rifle from 1583 and a board for the game of go with gold lacquer used by the warlords Toyotomi Hideyoshi and Tokugawa Ieyasu. Dry landscapes are tucked into the interstices of the building. The Totekiko Garden is claimed to be the country's smallest and has rocks representing drops of water which have fallen into the sea— an expression of the individual's immersion in the infinite. The A-Un (Aum) Garden consists of two rock settings illustrating how opposites (in this case inhalation and exhalation) are inseparable and essentially one. In the words of the temple, "A-Un shows the truth of the universe and the essence of Zen."

Above The central erect stone of the Ryogintei Garden represents Sumeru, the mountain at the center of the universe in Buddhist cosmology. The surrounding sea is represented by moss.
Above left The path from the Abbot's Quarters to the tea house is formed of *tobi-ishi* (literally 'flying stones' or 'skipping stones'). Notice the large 'step-off' stone that acts as a transition between room and garden.
Right Polished floorboards in the Abbot's Quarters, a building that was constructed in 1502 and is thought to be the oldest in the Daitoku-ji complex.
Opposite below Despite its compact size, the Tokeitei Garden has rippled wave patterns which can be imagined as a vast ocean.

DAISEN-IN 大仙院
A 'Stream of Life' Rock Garden
FOUNDED 1509

The subtemple boasts an astonishing dry landscape, architecture of world renown, artwork by celebrated painters, a self-directed commentary in English and a jocular priest who likes to do on-the-spot calligraphy. Small wonder, then, that Daisen-in is such a popular place with visitors. Moreover, it is alive with history, for famed tea master Sen no Rikyu served supremo Hideyoshi here and Zen master Takuan Soho gave instruction here to the swordsman Miyamoto Musashi.

Appreciation of the subtemple is deepened by awareness of the historical significance, and

DAISEN-IN AT A GLANCE

Founded 1509 by priest Kogaku Soko (posthumously Daisho Kokushi). 'Subtemple of the Great Immortals'

Affiliation Daitoku-ji School of Rinzai Zen

Special features Oldest Hojo and *tokonoma*, outstanding dry landscape, tea room used by Sen no Rikyu

Opening 9 am–5 pm (¥400); English booklet (¥500); green tea set (¥400)

Zazen Sat, Sun 5 am–6 pm; Dec–Feb 4.30 am–5.30 pm; Instruction and tea (¥1000); call in advance

Event Early/mid-March: Kokei-ki for the third abbot; tea served (¥1000)

Access Northern part of Daitoku-ji. Bus 206 to Daitoku-ji mae, then 5 mins walk

Contact (075) 491-8346

the English-language booklet offers excellent value. It highlights the changes in design at the time of the subtemple's foundation, particularly the move from wooden shutters to paper window screens (*shoji*) and sliding panels (*fusuma*). The use of tatami mats was also an innovation, replacing straw mats that were folded up for storage (*tatamu* means 'to fold').

At the heart of the subtemple stands the Abbot's Quarters, and it is worth noting the *genkan* (entrance area), introduced from China and the first of its kind in Japan. In the northern corner, a prized tea room houses an early example of the *tokonoma*. When tea maestro Sen no Rikyu served tea here, he collaborated with nature by simply laying a ladle across the hollow top of a rock for use as a wash basin.

The altar room houses stunning artwork, which illustrates the move from ink to color in the sixteenth century. The dreamy landscapes painted by Soami (1472–1525) contrast with the nature paintings of Kano Motonobu (1476–1559), whose birds have detail and individuality.

For most visitors, however, it is the dry landscape garden that commands attention. Laid out by the founder, it features a 'stream of life' that runs round the sides of the Abbot's Quarters. Based on the Chinese tradition of Mt Horai, where dwell the Daoist Immortals, the stream issues forth vigorously at first, rushing over obstacles before emptying into an ocean of oblivion, which can be viewed at leisure from the veranda of the Main Hall. The expanse of raked sand is interrupted only by two purifying cones, which represent the overcoming

Above Leaves of a bodhi tree outside the main garden wall, the same kind of tree under which the Buddha became enlightened.

Opposite The stream of life which issues forth from a group of rocks representing Mt Horai flows around the Main Hall and grows calm before entering into the Sea of Emptiness. The two purifying cones of sand are set in front of the entranceway into the hall.

of ego and delusion. In the corner, a sal tree speaks to the shortness of life through the brevity of its flowers (Buddha died beneath such a tree). Taken overall, the dry garden is a masterpiece of allusion, ending with emptiness but suggestive of so much.

ZUIHO-IN 瑞峯院

Two Striking Rock Gardens

FOUNDED 1546

Zuiho-in is the smallest of the Daitoku-ji subtemples open to the public but it has much to offer. The chief attractions are two remarkable gardens designed in the 1960s by Mirei Shigemori (1896–1975). Unexpectedly, one has a strong Christian theme and is shaped like a cross. This is because the founder, Kyushu warlord Otomo Sorin (1530–87), converted from Zen to Catholicism at forty-eight during the Warring States period. The conversion had military advantages; by allying with the Jesuits he gained access to Portuguese merchant ships and their weapons.

The approach to the subtemple is through a semi-formal garden of pine and cedar trees. Before reaching the entrance, the path makes three distinct turns to provide a sense of distance. Laid out along the side of the Main Hall is the first of the Shigemori gardens, the Garden of Solitary Meditation, with vigorous, almost violent waves carved out of raked sand. These are complemented by dynamic upright stones representing mythical Mt Horai, from which a peninsula stretches suggestively towards an individual rock, bereft and all at sea.

At the far end, a line of stepping stones leads, daringly, across the sea of sand to a tea room (unthinkable in a traditional tea garden, where a sense of separateness is provided by fence, bushes and trees). The innovative side of Shigemori is evident, too, in his other garden, which is laid out in the form of a crucifix. To see it clearly, the viewer needs to stand on the walkway, directly behind which is a stone lantern with a Virgin Mary buried at its base. It is an indication of the inclusiveness of Zen. From its very beginnings, Buddhism embraced Hindu deities, and during its time in China it incorporated elements of Daoism. Here at Zuiho-in the imagery of Christianity is integrated into the very fabric of the subtemple.

ZUIHO-IN AT A GLANCE

Founded 1546 by the *daimyo* Otomo Sorin; founding priest Tesshu Sokyu. 'Subtemple of Zuiho' (Buddhist name of Otomo Sorin)

Affiliation Daitoku-ji School of Rinzai Zen

Special features Two Shigemori gardens, Christian connections

Opening 9 am–5 pm (¥400)

Access Bus 206 to Daitoku-ji mae, then 5 mins walk

Contact (075) 491-1454

Above Shigemori's tribute to the converted temple founder consists of a barely discernible abstract cross, in reference to the period of Hidden Christians. (The two rocks in the foreground indicate the central axis, with the cross point indicated by a rock in the top left and its counterpart in the moss to the right.)

Left Water bowls for rinsing hands on the way to tea ceremonies can play an important decorative role, as here in this unusual creation.

Opposite top Vigorous wave patterns give a feeling of turbulence to Mirei Shigemori's Horai garden.

Left Unconventionally, the stepping stones to a tea house are here set in the same dry landscape as one featuring the layout of a cross.

Right In the south-facing garden, known as Dokuzatei (Sitting Alone Garden), a lone rock stands as solitary outpost to a rocky promontory, emphasizing individual isolation.

KOTO-IN 高桐院

A Sumptuous Garden and Stunning Maple Colors

FOUNDED 1601

Koto-in is a very special space. Although it is overrun with visitors in autumn because of the stunning maple colors, for much of the rest of the year it is a haven of peace. It was created as a refuge for Hosokawa Tadaoki, a world-weary warrior who was also a cultivated aesthete. Such was his religious devotion that in later life he became a Zen priest. His family crest was the paulownia, hence the subtemple's name.

The approach leads along a paved walkway alive with orange hues when the maple leaves turn. The veranda of the main building looks onto a sumptuous moss garden, in which a

Top The entrance path is a master-piece of spatial design and extends for nearly two-thirds of the temple grounds.
Below In the main garden a single stone lantern acts as focal point amongst the moss and maples. To complement contemplation, *matcha* green tea is served on the veranda.

solitary stone lantern blends into the surrounds. The soothing nature of the greenery is best appreciated with a bowl of tea, appropriate for a subtemple that historically has strong tea connections.

 Prior to his war service, Tadaoki had been one of the Seven Disciples of tea master Sen no Rikyu. He built the Shokoken tea room for Hideyoshi's grand tea party of 1588, and he used wood from Rikyu's residence to make the subtemple's study. The neighbor-ing tearoom has a 'crawling entrance' (*nijiriguchi*), which Tadaoki himself is credited with creating in order to compel humility and the removal of swords. Outside stands a magnificent wash basin hollowed from a large rock plundered from the Korean Imperial Palace.

The small cemetery not only contains the grave of Tadaoki but also of his famous wife, Hosokawa Gracia (1563–1600). Hers was a tragic life, for as the daughter of the man who killed Nobunaga, she lived all her life under suspicion. Moreover, she converted to Christianity at a time when it was in disfavor, and she chose to die rather than fall into the hands of her husband's enemies. The stone lantern by her grave was treasured by Sen no Rikyu as Tenka-ichi (World's Best), but at the back a large piece has been broken off, apparently out of spite by Rikyu when Hideyoshi demanded possession. Now it serves as a prized imperfection in a setting that could be considered perfect.

KOTO-IN AT A GLANCE

Founded 1601 by the general Hosokawa Tadaoki. 'Subtemple of the Tall Paulownia'

Affiliation Daitoku-ji School of Rinzai Zen

Special features Tea houses, moss garden, maples

Opening 9 am–5 pm (¥400); green tea set (¥400)

Event Oct, 2nd Sun: special showing of treasures (¥500)

Access Bus 206 to Daitoku-ji mae, then 5 mins walk

Contact (075) 492-0068

This prized water basin (*tsukubai*) was carved out of a rock seized from the Korean Imperial Palace by temple founder Hosokawa Tadaoki.

The stepping stone path leads to the Shokoken, one of two tea houses at the temple. Tadaoki was a keen practitioner of tea and one of the Seven Disciples of Sen no Rikyu.

A great attraction of Japanese temples is the way *fusuma* screen doors open up to frame a scene of nature. Here a stone path beckons entry into the three-dimensional composition.

MYOSHIN-JI AT A GLANCE

Founded 1342 by Kanzan Egen. 'Temple of the Exceptional Mind'

Affiliation Head of Myoshin-ji School of Rinzai Zen (46 subtemples, over 3,400 branch temples)

Special features Abbot's Quarters, Lecture Hall, steam baths, subtemples

Opening Grounds (free); guided tour every 20 mins 9 am–4 pm except midday (¥500)

Accommodation Shunko-in (Eng); Daishin-in and Torin-in (Jp); Hanazono Kaikan

Zazen Sat/Sun, not Aug, 5.30 pm–9 am, overnight in *dojo* (¥2000). Also every month 7th and 8th, 6 am–8 pm with talk (¥500)

Events Aug 9–10: Oshoro-mukae lantern festival in the Hatto; Nov 3–4, 9 am–3.30 pm: Bakuryo-ten, airing of treasures (¥1000)

Access 5 mins walk from JR Hanazono Station; bus to Myoshinji-mae

Contact (075) 463-3121 (www.myoshinji.or.jp/english/)

MYOSHIN-JI 妙心寺
A Monastical World of Its Own
FOUNDED 1342

Myoshin-ji is the biggest of all Rinzai Zen's forty monasteries. Indeed, it has more than half of all Rinzai's branch temples. Within its walled complex the warren of small streets resembles a medieval village. Open gateways give onto picturesque front gardens, many of which are centuries old. These are ranged around a monastic core of massive wooden buildings. It is a prime example of the classic Zen temple layout. From the middle of the Imperial Messenger's Gate, a central axis runs north through the Lotus Pond, Sanmon gate, Buddha Hall and Lecture Hall, finishing at the entrance to the Abbot's Quarters.

Right Hydrangea found in sub-temple gardens blooms during the rainy season in June and is associated with deep feelings, such as heartfelt gratitude.
Far left The pine tree is a symbol of endurance for its ability to remain evergreen in the depths of winter.
Left The kitchen, called *kuri* at Zen temples, was built in 1653. Meals were prepared here for the abbot and guests, with a refectory able to cater for up to 500. The building also houses a Buddhist altar and temple offices (not open to the public).

Like other Kyoto temples, Myoshin-ji suffered terrible destruction during the Onin War (1467–77), and the present buildings date from rebuilding between the fifteenth and seventeenth centuries. Entry is restricted, save for a guided tour that allows access to the Abbot's Quarters, Lecture Hall and Bathhouse. Although the tour is in Japanese, the items can be admired for themselves without the need for explanation.

Temple Tour

The ticket office is in the Abbot's Quarters (O-hojo), and while waiting one can inspect the altar room with its Amida statue over 1,000 years old. The black ink *sumi-e* paintings of mountains and temples are by master artist Kano Tanyu (1602–74), and to either side hang banners with guidelines for living, such as this:

Once a day sit quietly and settle your heart and mind. In the realization that humans are precious, give importance to yourself and others. In gratitude for the gift of life, return the favor by showing kindness to others.

The formidable Lecture Hall (Hatto) can hold up to a thousand people and is supported by eighteen huge pillars standing freely on stone bases. The cavernous space is dominated by a raised platform from which the abbot delivers his Dharma lecture. In one corner stands Japan's oldest bell, inscribed 698, but now out of commission owing to a crack. Tourists are invited to listen to a recording of its highly prized ringing tone.

On the ceiling is a *Dragon in the Cloud*, a stunning creation by the seventeenth-century genius Kano Tanyu, which alone makes the tour worthwhile. The picture was three years in the planning, and the artist mixed the paint himself from a variety of plants and shells. The result is a dragon that appears to be ascending or descending, depending on the viewpoint. It is enclosed within a circle representing the universe, and its eye is positioned dead center so that its protective gaze follows the observer around the room.

The tour concludes with entry into the old Bathhouse, built in 1656 and used by monks until 1927. It operated like a modern sauna, with two ovens for boiling water that was poured onto a metal tub to create steam in the wooden cabin above. The facility could hold six people at a time and was used as a form of religious practice, with monks sitting in meditation for the length of a burning incense stick.

The *sarasoju* (sal tree), also known as *natsu tsubaki* (summer camellia), has flowers that fall off within fifteen hours of opening. This makes it a symbol of transience, which is why the tree is included in pictures of Buddha on his deathbed (known as Nehan-zu). At Torin-in is a sal tree garden open to the public in June, and each morning priests remove blossoms that have wilted or turned brown.

KANZAN EGEN (1277–1360)

Myoshin-ji owes its existence to the patronage of Emperor Hanazono (1297–1348). After his retirement, he became a 'cloistered emperor', devoted to the study of Buddhism and a disciple of Shuho Myocho, founder of Daitoku-ji. In 1335 he became a monk, and when he decided to turn part of his estate into a temple he invited his teacher to be the first abbot. The elderly master was in poor health, however, and suggested instead his disciple Kanzan Egen, at the time living as a hermit in the mountains of Gifu. Originally from Nagano, Egen had studied at Daitoku-ji before taking up a life of solitude at the age of fifty-three.

The new temple took its tone from Egen, who practiced austere poverty. His robe was made of rough fiber woven from wisteria vine, and such was his zeal that on numerous occasions he chased his own nephew out of the temple for insufficient devotion. The priority put on spiritual practice meant that building work was neglected, decoration overlooked and robes repaired rather than replaced. Indeed, the regime was so strict that few could tolerate it.

There are many stories about Egen's lack of concern for material matters. He once ordered a monk to prepare a hot bath for a visitor, and when the monk complained that there was not enough firewood, Egen told him to use the boards from the eaves. The frugal master lived to the ripe old age of eighty-three. "I ask only this of you. Dedicate yourselves to the Great Matter," were his parting words before dying.

Unlike Daitoku-ji, the temple did not become associated with 'worldly pursuits' such as landscape gardening and the tea ceremony. Even today, the training is said to be severe, with an emphasis on begging and physical labor (at the time of writing, some twenty monks are undergoing instruction). Another characteristic of the temple is that *koan* riddles are tailored to individual needs rather than following the standard progression. Over 600 years from its foundation, Egen's thinking continues to be a guiding influence in the life of the monastery.

Subtemples

Myoshin-ji has managed to retain more subtemples than any other monastery, though they are generally off-limits as they operate as family homes for the resident priests. At the time of writing, only three are open year-round (see Keishun-in and Daishin-in below and Taizo-in on page 96). Many subtemples leave the gate open for parishioners, meaning that their front gardens can be viewed. Some have special openings or allow visitors to attend annual events. Daiho-in, open in spring and autumn, has a fine tea garden, with tea sets available on the veranda. Torin-in hosts several annual events: Azuki kayu (bean porridge) January 15–31 (¥3500); in early May and October there is a Lantern Festival (¥500); and in late June to July viewing of sal flowers with *shojin ryori* temple food (¥5950).

Keishun-in (8 am–5 pm; ¥400) was founded in 1598 and, unusually for Myoshin-ji, has a tea house and garden, obscured from view by foliage. Together with the Study, it was

relocated in 1631 from Nagahama Castle. There is also a stroll garden, a dry landscape garden and some seventeenth-century paintings by members of the Kano School. A green tea set is served in a room with a *tokonoma* alcove, which with the sliding doors removed gives a sense of integration into the surrounding greenery.

Daishin-in (9 am–4 pm), founded in 1492 by the powerful Hosokawa family, provides a rare opportunity to experience old-style accommodation (tel. 075 461-5714; ¥5000). Facilities are basic, with futon, paper screens and shared toilets, but this is a true Zen atmosphere with rooms looking onto dry landscape gardens and a shojin ryori breakfast. The temple boasts modern gardens created in the 1950s by Kinsaku Nakane. In front of the Abbot's Quarters is cut stone and white sand lined by peonies, and in front of the Studio is a garden consisting of seventeen stones arranged in moss and white sand to represent a dragon.

The dry landscape at Daishin-in has gracefully curved banks of moss abutting a white gravel 'river' which is laid out in front of the tea room and overlooked by the temple lodging house (*shukubo*).

Myoshin-ji is a warren of walled lanes, giving it a medieval atmosphere. It makes the monastery a popular setting for historical drama. Although most of the subtemples are off-limits, some leave their gates open and visitors can get a glimpse of their front gardens.

TAIZO-IN 退蔵院
A Stroll Garden for all Seasons
FOUNDED 1404

The west garden, featuring a dry waterfall in a sea of raked gravel, has been attributed to sixteenth-century artist Kano Motonobu.

The yin–yang pair of gardens has dark sand for its yin side and light for the yang. The attributes of yin that link it to darkness include night-time, moon, water, winter, passivity and death.

Taizo-in is the most popular of Myoshin-ji's subtemples open to the public. It is also the oldest subtemple in the complex, founded in 1404 after a feudal lord was converted to Zen by the abbot of Myoshin-ji. It is known for its gardens, which comprise both dry landscape and pond as well as traditional and modern. In addition, it has a most curious painting, *Catching a Catfish with a Gourd*, by Josetsu (1405–96), a Chinese immigrant who introduced *sumi-e* ink painting to Japan.

Josetsu's picture, one of Japan's earliest surviving ink paintings, shows a barefooted old man fishing on a river bank. The stiffness of his body contrasts with other features, such as the water flow and slippery fish. The puzzle the picture poses is that the catfish is much too big to enter the narrow neck of the gourd. The painting seems designed to perplex, as if a visual *koan*. It was commissioned by the shogun Ashikaga Yoshimochi, and across the top are thirty-one poems on the subject by high-ranking Zen

priests. (The original is in the Kyoto National Museum and the subtemple displays a reproduction.)

To the west of the Abbot's Quarters is a rock garden designed by the artist Kano Motonobu (1476–1559), who lived for a while at the subtemple. In the dry water flow can be seen bridges, islands and a waterfall. The surrounding trees and bamboo grove are integrated into the composition, such that the secluded landscape has been called a 3D equivalent of the artist's ink paintings.

A modern stroll garden, Yoko-in, created in 1956 by Kinsaku Nakane (1917–95), occupies the rest of the grounds. The upper section consists of an unusual pairing of yin and yang rock gardens. The former has dark sand offset by a weeping cherry and a set of eight rocks (even numbers being yin). The yang garden complements it

TAIZO-IN AT A GLANCE

Founded 1404 by Hatano Shigemichi, a *daimyo* of Izumo. 'Subtemple of Accumulated Hidden Virtue'

Affiliation Myoshin-ji School of Rinzai Zen

Special features Rock garden, pool garden, painting of fishing with a gourd

Opening 9 am–5 pm (¥500); green tea set (¥500)

Zazen By arrangement for groups of 10 or more; also calligraphy, ikebana, tea ceremony, guided tour, *shojin-ryori*. (Reservations: see website below)

Event Late Sept: moon-viewing, tea and *shojin ryori* (¥9000) (reservations)

Access Next to the Myoshin-ji Sanmon gate (see Myoshin-ji for directions)

Contact (075) 463-2855 (www.taizoin.com/en/)

with seven rocks in a sea of light-colored sand against a background of Japanese cedars. In the lower section is a carp pond fed by a waterfall. Wooded surroundings, trimmed azalea bushes, shoreline plants and a wisteria arbor provide a lush scene that is constantly changing with the seasons. Here in these idyllic surrounds is the perfect place to sit and ponder the slippery matter of Josetsu's brain teaser: how exactly *do* you catch a catfish in a gourd?

The celebrated Yoko-in Garden is the creation of Kinsaku Nakane, notable twentieth-century designer. As the visitor moves through the stroll garden, different landscapes are revealed, with the path ending at a wisteria viewing area from which to contemplate the composition as a whole.

97

SHUNKO-IN 春光院
Lessons in Mindfulness

FOUNDED 1509

In recent years **Shunko-in** has won attention for reaching out to foreigners. It stands in contrast to the traditional image of Zen in Kyoto, which is known for its conservatism and exclusivism. However, Takafumi Kawakami, the American-educated son of the head priest, has been pioneering change, and Shunko-in presents a range of activities for foreigners which includes a Zen 'taster' of meditation, talk and guided tour. There is also the possibility of staying overnight in purpose-built accommodation.

Kawakami majored in religious studies at Arizona State University, and since returning to Japan has assumed the post of Deputy Head of the subtemple, teaching Zen in English to over 5,000 people a year. His focus is on mindfulness, the mental benefits of sitting *zazen*, and its application to everyday life. He has led workshops, given lectures and is often featured in the media in Japan. He has also spoken out as a LGBT activist, unusual in the conformist world of Japan, and is happy to perform same-sex weddings at the temple.

Shunko-in has several items of note. Founded in 1590, it was built by a

In front of the Abbot's Quarters, the Sazareishi Garden makes reference to the Grand Shrines of Ise. Raked gravel and rocks represent islands in Ise Bay, beyond which stands the Forest of Naiku (Inner Shrine) and the Geku (Outer Shrine). The temple's seventeenth-century patron, Ishikawa Noriyuki, oversaw the Ise region, and like others of his time believed in a combinatory form of Shinto-Buddhism.

feudal lord of the Matsue area to honor his oldest son killed in battle. As well as nineteenth-century paintings by Kano Eigaku (1790–1867), there is an attractive dry landscape that symbolizes the Ise Grand Shrine and a grove dedicated to the Shinto sun goddess Amaterasu. The temple also houses a church bell and stone lantern from the era of Hidden Christians. More recently, it was home for a while to the mid-twentieth century philosopher Shinichi Hisamatsu, whose friend D. T. Suzuki often came to visit. It is said the azaleas in the front garden were planted by the pair of influential Zen thinkers.

Unlike other temples and sub-temples covered in this book, Shunko-in is not normally open to visitors except by reservation for its special activities. Details can be found on its English-language website.

Above The place in the altar room from where the priest kneels to recite sutras and perform ceremonies. To the right, a *mokugyo* drum carved in the shape of a fish is struck with a soft mallet to keep time during sutra chanting. To the left, the *keisu* gong is struck with a padded mallet.
Below Zen temples are storehouses of artwork and artifacts. This is an old *taiko* drum found in storage at Shunko-in. Amongst the temple's other treasures is a sixteenth-century bell from Kyoto's first Christian church.
Opposite top Cushions are set out for a group of visitors interested to learn more about the Zen style of meditation.

SHUNKO-IN AT A GLANCE

Founded 1590 by the feudal lord Horio Yoshiharu. 'Subtemple of the Ray of Spring Light'

Affiliation Myoshin-ji School of Rinzai Zen

Special features *Zazen*, talk and guided tour, 90 mins (¥2500); accommodation, *zazen* and tour (¥6500 + tax)

Opening Schedule varies; check shunkoin.com for details

Zazen Morning drop-in sessions (see website). Groups by arrangement

Access In the Myoshin-ji complex, northwest of the Daihojo (main hall)

Contact (075) 462-5488 (www.shunkoin.com/)

TENRYU-JI 天龍寺
The Original 'Borrowed Landscape' Garden

FOUNDED 1339

Tenryu-ji was once Kyoto's leading Zen temple, with extensive grounds and 150 subtemples. It dominated the beautiful environs of Arashiyama where the aristocracy went on leisure outings. Ravaged by fire on no fewer than eight separate occasions, it was rebuilt most recently in Meiji times while retaining the original style. The temple was particularly badly hit by the religious reforms of the era, meaning that it lost nine-tenths of its grounds. The chief pride, the Sogenchi Garden, is the only feature to date back to the original foundation, and it played a key role in the inclusion of Tenryu-ji as part of the World Heritage Site of Ancient Kyoto, the only Zen temple to be so honored.

The origins of the temple lie in the power struggle of the Northern and Southern Courts period (1334–92), when Japan had rival emperors. It began when the warlord Ashikaga Takauji turned on his ally, Emperor Go-Daigo, forcing him into exile and assuming the title of shogun. When Go-Daigo died five years later, Ashikaga Tadayoshi (the shogun's younger brother) had a vision of a golden dragon rising from a river, which Zen master Muso Soseki (1275–1351) interpreted in mythological terms as the late emperor's vengeful spirit. Accordingly, he persuaded the shogun to build a temple of appeasement.

To finance the project, Soseki sought the backing of the influential Tadayoshi for a trading mission to China. It proved a big success, and in subsequent years the Tenryu-ji Ship contributed greatly to the growth of Zen in Kyoto through the import of religious and cultural items. By 1386 the temple had assumed first place in the city's Gozan system.

Because of the topography, the approach to the temple, unusually, is from the east. It leads past the temple's oldest structure, the Choku-shimon (Imperial Messenger's Gate). The subtemples that line the pathway are closed to the public, although their carefully tended front

Above Temple gardens provide habitat to songbirds, prominent among them the *mejiro* (Japanese white-eye), which feeds on nectar from the plum trees that line Tenryu-ji's stone walls.

Right The Sogenchi Garden, chief pride of the monastery, retains the original design featuring Mt Kameyama as 'borrowed scenery'. Focal points are provided by a rocky peninsula and a pine tree shaped as a 'drooping dragon head'. The reflections in the mirror pond serve to illustrate the unity of heaven, human and nature.

MUSO SOSEKI (1275–1351)

Muso Soseki is one of Zen's most important figures, who combined spirituality with artistry and who achieved excellence in fields such as poetry, calligraphy and garden design. As well as being the founding abbot of Tenryu-ji, he was also the creator of gardens at Saiho-ji and Toji-in. Moreover, he wrote books on Buddhism and was an influential figure in the Gozan system. He lived at a pivotal time for Zen in Japan, as it moved from dependency on Chinese masters to native teachers, and with numerous followers of his own he played a vital role in the transition.

In his youth, Soseki studied Esoteric Buddhism but converted to Zen at nineteen after witnessing the agonizing death of a teacher famed for his learning. It made him realize the importance of practice rather than the acquisition of knowledge. "I had been misguided a long time," he wrote. "It seems I was seeking heaven by digging in the ground." Amongst his teachers was a Chinese monk at Kencho-ji in Kamakura, and in 1335 he became enlightened following a long session of *zazen* sitting meditation.

For the next twenty years Soseki lived in seclusion with a few companions in the northern provinces. Such was his reputation that he was forced to move to escape attention, and he even turned down invitations from the emperor and shogunate. Eventually, however, under pressure from Emperor Go-Daigo he accepted the post of abbot of Nanzen-ji.

In 1339, Soseki was invited to convert the Pure Land temple of Saiho-ji into a Zen monastery, and his garden design became an important model for later creations. After the death of Go-Daigo that year, Soseki was appointed founding abbot of Tenryu-ji and was also involved in setting up the Ashikaga family temple of Toji-in, where he created another masterpiece (see page 104). In *Dialogues in a Dream*, he wrote of the different uses such gardens serve. "There are those who regard mountains, rivers, grass, trees, tiles, and stones to be their own Original Nature," he wrote. "Their love for gardens may resemble worldly affection, but they employ that affection in their aspiration for the Way." (tr. Kirchner)

gardens are on display. The Lotus Pond is a big draw in July when its flowers bloom, since Tenryu-ji has one of the best such displays among Kyoto's Zen temples (the lotus is symbolic of enlightenment because of its ability to produce pure beauty from out of muddy depths).

Sogenchi Garden

There are two routes for visitors, one that skirts the pond garden and its surrounds, and one with shoes off through the inside of the buildings.

The Lecture Hall (Hatto) has an altar statue of Shakyamuni, the historical Buddha, flanked by his attendants Fugen and Monju. On the low ceiling is a 'Cloud Dragon' painted in 1997 by *nihonga* artist Matazo Kayama, commissioned for the 650th anniversary of Muso Soseki's death. It consists of 159 lacquered cypress planks, one inch thick, on which a layer of plaster was applied to form a circle enclosing the 'all-seeing' dragon.

The Abbot's Quarters (Hojo) comprise a large open tatami room

that can be divided by sliding *fusuma* doors. Beyond lies the Sogenchi (Pond of the Well-Spring of Happiness), which was designed for contemplative viewing from the veranda. The craggy shorelines and peninsula with rocky islets recall earlier Heian gardens, but the static vantage point, with the 'borrowed scenery' of Mt Arashiyama and Ogura in the background, was an innovative feature that influenced later gardens.

The pond's principle feature is a grouping of seven vertical rocks (seven

The Abbot's Quarters consist of a huge tatami space whose sliding doors open up to frame the Sogenchi Garden. Created in the fourteenth century, the garden has long been a celebrated sight and was featured in an early guide to the city in 1799.

Hogon-in is noted for its 600-year-old garden and for the fine examples of the art of bamboo fencing. Usually rocks are moved to fit the garden design, but here the garden was shaped around the rocks *in situ*. Moss-lined paths lead around them, and special features include a hill representing Mt Sumeru, center of the Buddhist cosmology, and a boat-shaped rock for travel between worlds (rocks being a symbol of the eternal). These are complemented by reference to the cycle of birth and death, with the garden design highlighting the new growth of spring and the changing colors of autumn.

being a special number in Daoism). There is also a stone bridge, said to be the oldest of its kind, and a dry Dragon Waterfall, before which stands a rock representing the carp that in Chinese mythology wanted to turn into a dragon by leaping the falls—a symbol of the success that comes from endeavor.

From the Abbot's Quarters a covered corridor runs to a memorial hall known as Tahoden, dedicated to appeasing Go-Daigo whose statue it contains. The adjacent garden path leads up a slope on the far side of the pond, where shrubs and maples add seasonal color to the landscaped grounds. The foliage obscures the pond below, offering discrete glimpses, and though these days crowds may intrude, it is possible to imagine the sublime serenity of former times.

Subtemples

Two of Tenryu-ji's subtemples have special openings in spring and autumn (entrance ¥500; *matcha* tea ¥500).

Kogen-ji was founded in 1429 and originally stood at the foot of Mt Ogura, but was relocated to its present position in 1884 with views of Mt Arashiyama. Paintings, poems and statues are on display, and attention is drawn to the marks in a wooden pillar made by the Choshu clan while testing their swords in pre-Restoration days.

TENRYU-JI AT A GLANCE

Founded 1339 by shogun Ashikaga Takauji; founding priest Muso Soseki. 'Temple of the Heavenly Dragon'

Affiliation Head of Tenryu-ji School of Rinzai (13 subtemples, 104 branch temples)

Special features Sogenchi Garden, ceiling dragon, Tahoden (memorial hall), Chokushimon Gate, Lotus Pond, *shojin ryori* at Shigetsu restaurant (¥3000–¥7000; reservation (075) 882-9725)

Opening hours 8.30 am–5 pm (¥500 for grounds, ¥600 for grounds and inside)

Zazen 2nd Sun (except Feb): open *zazenkai* 9–10 am followed by talk, in Yuun-an (free; reservation unnecessary)

Access 3 mins walk from Arashiyama Randen or 10 mins from Hankyu Station

Contact Tel: (075) 881-1235 (www.tenryuji.com)

TOJI-IN 等持院

A Soothing Sanctuary

FOUNDED 1341

Above The Seiren-tei tea house dating back to the fifteenth century overlooks the pond garden from the man-made Moon Hill (Tsukiyama). The path around the pond passes close to the tea house so visitors can inspect the *wabi-sabi* materials and craftsmanship.
Left Visitors to Toji-in are greeted by the fearsome features of Bodhi-dharma, known in Japan as Daruma. His stern expression serves as an example of gritty determination and perseverance. This modern portrait was painted by noted artist Seki Bokuo (1903–91), former abbot of Tenryu-ji to which Toji-in is affiliated.

Toji-in is one of Kyoto's best-kept secrets. It is close to popular tourist sights yet overlooked by passing crowds, so the delightful pond garden affords a rare chance for contemplative viewing. Established by the first of the Ashikaga shoguns, it served as a family temple for the ruling dynasty. The founding abbot was the influential Muso Soseki (page 102), and it was he who designed the delightful grounds. (The temple is administered by Tenryu-ji and has no resident priest.)

On entering, visitors are greeted by a striking portrait of Daruma by a former abbot of Tenryu-ji, and the stern face is a reminder of the gritty resolve required in Zen. The garden, on the other hand, speaks of repose, and is best viewed from the veranda of the Main Hall (where tea can be taken). The Heart-Shaped Pond, as its name suggests, is laid out in the form of the Chinese character for *shin* (heart-mind). The extensive rock work and shrubbery are dominated by a curved red pine, and a flat stone bridge leads to Mt Horai, mythical Isle of the Blessed.

The soothing sound of the feeder stream is complemented by the movement of carp in the pond, while to the left the eye is drawn upwards to a thatched tea house atop a small slope. Named Seiren-tei (Hut of Pure Ripples), it would once have looked onto Mt Kinugusa, though the vista is sadly blocked off now by the buildings of Ritsumeikan University.

Garden slippers are provided for visitors, and it is possible to follow the path around the pond to a wooded area at the far end. Along the way are carefully placed plants and shrubs as

TOJI-IN AT A GLANCE

Founded 1341 by shogun Ashikaga Takauji; founding priest Muso Soseki. 'Sub-temple of Focussed Meditation' (from Ashikaga Takauji's posthumous name)

Affiliation Tenryu-ji School of Rinzai Zen

Special features Pond garden, tea house, Daruma painting, mortuary statues of shoguns

Opening hours 10 am–5 pm (¥500); *matcha* tea set (¥500)

Access 10 mins from Ritsumeikan stop, city bus 50, or Randen Toji-in Station.

Contact 075 461-5786.

well as different kinds of moss. Seasonal changes add to the charm: in spring flowering camellias and azaleas, in autumn the fragrance of *mokusei* and the changing colors of the maples. On the south side is the grave of the founder, Ashikaga Takauji (1305–58), while to the north the path leads up to

the tea house where one can inspect the rustic simplicity (*wabi-sabi*).

The Reikoden (Hall of Sacred Light) holds a collection of mortuary statues for the Ashikaga shoguns, who sit cross-legged facing inwards as if fixed forever in contemplation of the afterlife. Stylized and similar, they each carry a *shaku* symbol of authority and have Confucian-style pointed beards. Some have individual touches, for instance, the short but stern 13th shogun.

The object of worship is Riun Jizo, who mediates between worlds, flanked on one side by Bodhidharma, founder of Zen, and on the other by Muso Soseki, founder of the temple. The building speaks to the Muromachi period when Ashikaga rule marked the apogee of Zen influence in Japan. "All things must pass," runs the saying. Shogunal rule, too.

The pond garden as seen from the Shoin, or Study Room. The garden comprises two sections, one in which the pond is shaped like the Chinese character for *shin* (heart-mind), and one in which it takes the shape of a lotus flower.

Saiho-ji (Kokedera) 西芳寺

Kyoto's Most Famous Moss Garden

FOUNDED 1339

Garden enthusiasts come to Saiho-ji from far and wide, for its moss garden is said to be the most beautiful in Japan. Steve Jobs and Richard Gere are just two of the celebrities to have visited. Yet the temple is the most troublesome, and expensive, to access in Kyoto (applications are required in advance by *ofuku hagaki,* return postcard). The purpose is to limit the number of visitors since the moss is a delicate plant and adversely affected by human traffic. Despite the complications, those who visit find it well worth the trouble.

Before entering the garden, visitors are required to copy out Zen's main scripture, the Heart Sutra. It is considered a form of religious practice (tracing paper is provided). There is also chanting with bell and *mokugyo* drum by the father and son pair of priests who run the temple. This takes place in the Main Hall, built in 1969, which allows visitors to experience something of the Zen style of worship. (It is advisable not to spend too long on the sutra copying as visiting time is restricted to an hour and a half.)

The site was originally occupied by an ancient temple, which by the fourteenth century had fallen into disuse. Muso Soseki (1275–1351), founder of Tenryu-ji, was invited to convert it into a Zen temple, and he laid out the grounds with a lower pond

Moss is a delicate plant, easily damaged by direct sunlight. The shade provided by the tree canopy is a blessing not only for the moss but for summer visitors.

Stepping stones to a tea house are perfectly complemented by the moss in which they are set. It was scenes such as this that led to the tea garden being dubbed *roji* (dewy path).

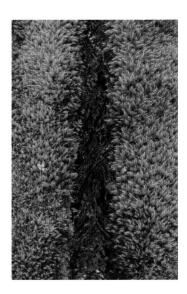

According to recent thinking, the garden only became covered in moss following flooding in the nineteenth century. This created the moist conditions in which the plant thrives.

garden and an upper dry section. The design proved hugely influential, becoming the model for such notable estates as those at the Gold and Silver Pavilions.

The pond in the lower portion of the grounds is shaped in the form of the Chinese character for *shin* (heart-mind). This was originally surrounded by white sand and it was only in the nineteenth century, as a result of flooding, that the area became covered with moss. Now there is a seamless carpet of differing hues produced by the varied species (120 have been identified in all). The location by the Katsura River with its 95 percent humidity is conducive to the growth of the moss, which is shielded from direct sunlight by numerous trees. Carefully positioned rocks, plants and bridges make this a prime example of humans and nature working in tandem to produce a work of art.

The upper portion of the garden, more rugged and austere, is up a small incline at the top of which is a tea house and dry landscape representing a waterfall deep in the mountains. The garden here was refashioned out of the former temple's cemetery, adding a dimension of transience to the beauty of the scene below. 'Mortality' is thus written into the very fabric of the

garden, and a Meditation Rock used by Soseki himself allowed for contemplation of such matters. "People who understand that mountains, streams, earth, plants, trees and rocks are all one with the fundamental self can make these natural features part of their meditation," Soseki wrote. More than mere moss, the garden of Saiho-ji was intended to be a true revelation.

SAIHO-JI AT A GLANCE

Founded 8th c. possibly by Gyoki; 1339 revived by Muso Soseki. 'Temple of Western Fragrance' (known colloquially as the Moss Temple)

Affiliation Tenryu-ji School of Rinzai Zen

Special features Pond and stroll garden, 120 types of moss, sutra copying

Opening Reservation in advance by return postcard (¥3000), 90 mins. (For details, see www.insidekyoto.com, or www.saihoji-kokedera-reservation.com)

Access 20 mins walk from Matsuo Taisha Station (Hankyu Arashiyama); city bus to Kokederamichi

Contact (075) 391-3631

GENKO-AN 源光庵
Two Perspectives on the World
FOUNDED 1346

The aphorisms hung in *tokonoma* alcoves are usually taken from a book of notable Zen sayings, or Zengo. The five Chinese characters featured here translate as "A single drop spreads wide." The writing, which is changed monthly or seasonally, is typically done by the head abbot. Visitors kneel before the alcove to admire the calligraphy and contemplate the meaning.

Genko-an is known above all for a pair of windows: a square one named the Window of Confusion and a round one named the Window of Enlightenment. Both look onto the same garden but offer different perspectives. After paying respects at the altar, visitors sit before them contemplating the differences. Like a *koan* riddle, the effect is intended to jolt the mind into a deeper understanding of how perception is shaped. Somehow the view through the round window is more appealing, and the poet-singer Shinji Tanimura put his feelings into words:

This is what the round window
whispers:
Seasons change by color,
Colors change to emptiness.
Whatever meets the eye, I find,
Is always in a state of change.

The temple was originally founded as a Rinzai residence for a retired abbot of Daitoku-ji, and the change to Soto came about in 1694 after it had fallen into disuse. A reforming priest named Manzan Dohaku (1635–1715) from Kanazawa took over the temple: "He who rectified and renewed the Soto School" says a stone inscription.

His statue stands in the Founder's Hall, beneath which he lies buried.

Next to the reception is a set of rooms containing ink paintings by the Edo-era artist Yamaguchi Sekkei (1644–1732). The building abuts onto a busy dry landscape garden in which the outline of Turtle Island is clearly visible (its companion Crane Island has crumbled away). From here visitors proceed to the Main Hall where Japanese visitors can sometimes be seen gazing intently upwards. This is because of the so-called 'blood ceiling'.

In 1600, several hundreds of soldiers were massacred or committed suicide

The round 'window of enlightenment' and the square 'window of delusion' provide non-verbal instruction in Zen thinking, prompting the viewer to reflect on self and selflessness.

GENKO-AN AT A GLANCE

Founded 1346 by Tetsuo, abbot of Daitoku-ji; refounded 1694 by Manzan Dohaku. 'Hermitage of Original Radiance'

Affiliation Eihei-ji School of Soto Zen

Special features Two viewing windows, turtle–crane garden, blood-stained ceiling

Opening 9 am–5 pm (¥400)

Zazen 1st Sun each month, 7–9 am, including short talk in Jap (advance reservation)

Access Bus no. 6 to Takagamine Genkoan-mae, then 1 min, or underground to Kitao-ji Station, then 15 mins by bus

Contact 075-492-1858

The north garden has a backdrop of maples noted for the aesthetics of *komorebi* (the filtering of sunlight through leaves). The rock grouping center right is a Turtle Island. The matching Crane Island has not survived.

in Fushimi Castle in the southeast of Kyoto. Possibly 2,000 perished in all. Their sacrifice is said to have bought Tokugawa Ieyasu time to raise troops for the decisive Battle of Sekigahara, and the castle boards were subsequently dispersed for use in temples to soothe the souls of the dead. Four hundred years later, bloodstained prints remain visible (a handprint is clearly indicated in front of the round window). In this way, then, whether looking up or out, Genko-an gives pause for reflection on the greater matters of life—and death.

SHOKOKU-JI 相国寺
Perfecting the Art of Zen

FOUNDED 1383

Shokoku-ji was built as a shogunate showpiece and was intended to impress. It began as the personal project of Ashikaga Yoshimitsu, founder of the Golden Pavilion, with a location close to his Muromachi palace. To make space for the massive estate, locals were forced out of their homes. Construction took nine years to complete and involved the felling of Kyoto's oldest cedar and cypress trees. It held high status, ranking second among the Five Gozan temples and playing a prominent part in furthering Zen culture.

Over the centuries, Shokoku-ji accrued valuable assets, particularly ownership of the Golden and Silver Pavilions, which is why it is said to be the wealthiest of Kyoto's temples. As a consequence, it gives the appearance of being relatively unconcerned with attracting tourists. The only building normally open to the public is the museum, and even then it is best to check first as it is closed between exhibitions. The grounds, however, are free to wander around, and the greenery makes it a pleasant milieu in which to take in the atmosphere of a Zen temple. Here in the relatively small compound are housed no fewer than three shrines to Shinto *kami*. Here, too, are the head offices of the Joint Council for Rinzai and Obaku Zen.

The original layout is evident in the positioning of the lotus pond along a central axis on which stand the Lecture Hall (Hatto) and the Abbot's Quarters (Hojo). Noticeably missing are the Sanmon gate and Buddha Hall, both destroyed by fire in 1788 and never replaced. In their stead

Above The gentle curves of a bell-shaped window (*katomado*) provide a stylish first glimpse of the dry landscape in the Abbot's Quarters.
Right The red pine in front of the Lecture Hall (Hatto) is pruned so as not to obscure sight of the building. Both red and black pine are found at temples, the red with its softer needles being particularly attractive when catching the sunlight. Maintenance of the trees is done by hand, a skilled and time-consuming job.
Opposite The austere *karesansui* (dry landscape) in the Founder's Hall, open to the public for special occasions, has a restrained and formal air. The drainage area in the foreground is positioned beneath the edge of the hall roof. With its rock, pine tree, gateway and use of empty space, the scene is quintessentially Japanese.

SHOKOKU-JI AT A GLANCE

Founded 1383 by Ashikaga Yoshimitsu; founding priest (posthumously) Muso Soseki. 'Temple of the National Leader'

Affiliation Head of Shokoku-ji School of Rinzai Zen (13 subtemples, 121 branch temples)

Special features Museum (Hatto ceiling dragon), Hojo *fusuma* paintings rarely on display)

Opening Museum 10 am–4.30 pm (¥600); Hatto and Hojo occasional special openings

Zazen 2nd/4th Sun (not Aug) in the Kuri, 9–10 am, then talk in Jap (donation); also FAS Sats, 4–6 pm at Rinko-in (see FAS website)

Events Apr 8: Hanamatsuri (Buddha's b'day); Aug 2–3: Gyoten-koza *zazen* and lecture; Dec 31: ringing the New Year bell

Access Underground to Imadegawa Station, then 5 mins walk

Contact (075) 231-0301 (zen.rinnou.net)

Left The expanse of white gravel in the *hira-niwa* (flat garden) of the Abbot's Quarters is intended to reflect the moonlight at night, brightening the compound.
Below The rigid right angle of the garden is framed with a border of dark pebbles, emphasizing formality. The south-facing garden is used for entertaining guests of high standing.

are red pine trees, which give the precincts an open and wooded feel. Like other Buddhist temples, Shokoku-ji was severely hit by the reforms of Meiji times, when its sources of funding were cut by the government. In a sign of the times, much of the precinct had to be sold off to a Christian organization. Now the sprawling campus of Doshisha University surrounds two sides of the temple compound, shielding it from the hubbub of the main roads.

The Abbot's Quarters

The set of six tatami rooms in the Abbot's Quarters are only opened for special occasions. An ink painting by Gyokurin Shosui (1751–1814) of bamboo against a gold-leaf backing is intended to impress the arriving visitor by being placed at the entry point. The three rooms facing south, designed to entertain dignitaries, have paintings from the Imperial Palace with titles such as *Plum on Gold Leaf*. The northern set of three rooms for private use have ink paintings of Chinese sages

illustrating the notion that true wisdom lies in an intuitive identification with nature. On either side of the Abbot's Quarters lie dry landscape gardens, with that to the south being quietly formal and that in the north having a much more dramatic and individualized character.

From the Abbot's Quarters a covered corridor leads to the massive Lecture Hall (Hatto), built in 1605 and claimed as the oldest of its type. Statues of illustrious figures line the northern wall, including 'founding priest' Muso Soseki (1275–1351), who was awarded

the honor posthumously. On the ceiling is a painting of a *Dragon Glaring in Eight Directions*, whose eyes follow the visitor around the hall. Painted by Kano Mitsunobu (1565–1608), the young crouching creature is about to ascend to heaven to collect the ball of wisdom (normally grasped in the dragon's claws). Visitors are invited to clap their hands in the middle of the room in the hope of hearing the dragon's roar from on high in the reverberating echo.

The approach to the Jotenkaku Museum leads through an attractive

rock garden with unusual stone lanterns. Established in 1984 for the temple's 600th anniversary, it exhibits items from the Gold and Silver Pavilions along with calligraphy by past masters and treasured artwork, such as the folding screens of Hasegawa Tohaku (1539–1610). The museum also has an unusual tea room, the Muchu-an, built with wood that survived the burning of the Golden Pavilion in 1950.

The Art of Zen

The art school of Shokoku-ji was of great importance historically for it fostered the leading artists of Chinese ink painting in Japan. The founding figure was a Chinese immigrant named Josetsu, naturalized in 1370, who is known as 'the father of Japanese ink painting' (*suiboku*). He was one of the first practitioners of the new Zen style, and his best-known work, *Catching a Catfish with a Gourd*, is a whimsical illustration of a fisherman trying to catch a large fish, perhaps intended as a puzzle (see Taizo-in, page 96).

Among Josetsu's pupils was the monk Tensho Shubun (1414–63), who became director of the court painting bureau and whose Ten Ox-Herding Pictures are housed in the temple museum. He, in turn, was teacher to 'the genius of Chinese ink', Sesshu Toyo (1420–1506). Only twelve when he went to study at Shokoku-ji, the artist was a restless youth, always in a hurry to get on with his next drawing. One of the many stories about him relates how he was tied to a pillar as a form of discipline. The monk responsible was startled by a rat on his return to the

In the north garden of the Abbot's Quarters is a vigorous dry stream which serves as backdrop for informal gatherings and student instruction. The grounds are open to the public in spring and autumn.

room. It turned out, however, to be a life-like drawing done by the young novice with his foot in a pool of tears.

Sesshu was an experimentalist who enjoyed challenges, as a result of which his work shows mastery in different facets of ink painting, notably the harsh 'northern style' with its rugged strokes and the softer 'southern style' with rounded hills and misty features. Famous for pointillism and angular strokes, he created piercing mountain peaks and cascading waterfalls so vivid that they sear themselves into the mind of the viewer.

As he grew older, Sesshu moved away from Zen-inspired work to a more secular approach; there was greater realism, with added detail and color. The new trend was represented by painters from the samurai class, who were more inclined to sensual representation than the monk-artists

of Shokoku-ji with their idealized landscapes. The great era of Muromachi ink painting was drawing to a close, and in its museum Shokoku-ji treasures the legacy.

A later artist to be connected with the temple was Ito Jakuchu (1716–1800), creator of dazzling birds and plants. Born and bred in Kyoto, he took an interest in Zen and studied with the monk Daiten Kenjo, later abbot of Shokoku-ji. It was from him that Jakuchu received his artistic name, meaning 'like the void' in reference to the *Tao Te Ching*. The friendship gave the painter access to the temple's art collection, and he made such good use of it that he himself was to become a prized contributor. Jakuchu's grave lies in the temple cemetery, a fitting final resting place for it could be said that here at Shokoku-ji the art of Zen was truly perfected.

KINKAKU-JI 金閣寺
The Golden Pavilion

FOUNDED 1408

The first sight of the Golden Pavilion is thrilling. Maple trees obscure the view until a turn in the path reveals the building in all its glory. It is a dazzling vision of Amida's Pure Land (paradise) set in a carefully landscaped garden. It is bold and beautiful, it is a photographer's dream come true, but what does it have to do with Zen? Nothing could seemingly be further from the suppression of self, yet there is a strong spiritual aspect to the magnificence. Still today priests from Shokoku-ji come to hold rituals here.

For the apprentice in Yukio Mishima's novel *The Temple of the Golden Pavilion* (1956), the building is a mesmerizing edifice which holds him in thrall. Emotionally crippled and physically lame, he is tormented by its perfection: "When people concentrate on the idea of beauty, they are, without realizing it, confronted with the darkest thoughts that exist in this world." Eventually, he burns it to the ground—just as in real life a young monk burnt down the temple in 1950. The whole pavilion had to be rebuilt from scratch.

The building originated as part of a retirement estate for supremo Ashikaga Yoshimitsu (1368–94). Built on the site of an earlier villa, the estate was conceived on the grandest of scales with the pavilion just one of many structures. It functioned as a reliquary, and the glow of the gold leaf was thought to be spiritually purifying. On the second floor was a Buddha Hall with a shrine dedicated to Kannon, embodiment of Amida's compassion.

Top An ornamental bronze phoenix crowns the pavilion roof. The mythical bird is a Chinese symbol of heavenly favor, bestowing virtue, grace and happiness.

The Golden Pavilion is picturesque in all seasons, its beauty enhanced by the shimmering reflection. The plain wood of the ground floor, for welcoming guests, is topped by the gilded top floors which have a more spiritual orientation. The intention was to recreate a Buddhist paradise. "There are no fixed heavens and hells," said Kobo Daishi. "If you do good, gold and silver pavilions immediately appear."

Right In the grounds are two separate springs of fresh water used for making tea. The Ryumon-baku (Dragon Gate Waterfall) has a Carp Stone at the base which alludes to the Chinese legend of a fish struggling to ascend the falls to become a dragon. It is a lesson in perseverance to monks in their struggle to become enlightened.

Below The temple boasts more than the Golden Pavilion, for its Stroll Garden includes ponds, springs, tea houses, a small stone pagoda, a special style of bamboo fencing and a Shinto shrine for the spirit of place. (The temple buildings are not open to the public.)

(Yoshimitsu combined the practice of Zen with Pure Land belief, i.e. salvation through Amida.)

Following Yoshimitsu's death, the estate was turned into the Zen temple of Rokuon-ji (still the official name). During the Onin War (1467–77), the area was devastated and later it was again ravaged by fire, but fortuitously the Golden Pavilion survived. Architecturally, it combines three distinct styles. The first floor is in the aristocratic manner of Heian times and has a viewing area with verandas, unpainted wood and white plaster. A small fishing deck at the back has mooring for a boat. The two upper floors, more religious in orientation, are lacquered and covered in gold leaf. The second is in the *buke* style of the samurai, while the third is in the Zen style with arch-shaped windows. The shingled roof has a pyramid shape, rising to a top surmounted by a bronze

The camphor tree at the entrance dwarfs the immaculate temple wall with its five lines denoting imperial connection. Camphor trees are long-living, evergreen and have an insect-repelling fragrance. They produce bright green foliage in spring with small white flowers, and the wood contains essential oils used in medicine. By tradition, they are 'trees of the gods'.

The pavilion was rebuilt in 1955 after being burnt down, and in 1987 it was given a thicker layer of gold foil to increase the intensity of its sheen. The second floor, pictured here in the *buke-zukuri* (samurai residential style), contains paintings and religious statuary. It was used by Yoshimitsu for political and cultural discussions.

phoenix, Chinese symbol of social harmony.

The Stroll Garden is designed to open up different perspectives, while in the background the distant slopes of Mt Kinugasa extend the dimensional depth. The reflection in the Mirror Pond serves to intensify the other-worldly beauty by adding an air of unreality. The layout makes reference to famous sites in Chinese and Japanese literature, one example being a line of four stones in the water representing boats sailing for the mythical Isles of the Immortals.

Beyond the pond area is an Upper Garden, which is deliberately low key. Like Saiho-ji, which Yoshimitsu admired, it was built on a former cemetery, thereby linking the beauty of the grounds with transience and mortality. Amongst the features are the former abbot's living quarters, a spring used by Yoshimitsu for tea ceremonies, a temple hall housing a treasured Fudo-myo statue and a tea house added in the Edo period to enjoy views of the pavilion in the evening sun.

Once seen, the Golden Pavilion is not easily forgotten. There are places to enjoy a green tea set afterwards, and from within the tea bowl images of the pavilion may float to the surface, much as they haunted the mind of Mishima's protagonist. "Beauty is truth, truth beauty," wrote John Keats of a dimension in which spirituality intersects with art. His words might well be applied to the temple-pavilion, for here in this visionary creation is encapsulated the search for the sublime and the deep human desire for transcendence.

KINKAKU-JI AT A GLANCE

Founded 1408, with the conversion of Ashikaga Yoshimitsu's estate. 'Temple of the Golden Pavilion' (official name Rokuon-ji)

Affiliation Shokoku-ji School of Rinzai Zen

Special features Three-storey pavilion, pond and stroll garden

Opening 9.00–5.00 (¥400)

Access Subway to Kitaoji, then taxi (10 mins, about ¥1000) or bus (¥230)

Contact (075) 461-0013

GINKAKU-JI 銀閣寺
The Silver Pavilion

FOUNDED 1490

The Silver Pavilion is one of Kyoto's top tourist sights offering a sublime mix of Japanese garden and traditional architecture. The original estate, thirty times the present size, was established by the aesthete-shogun Ashikaga Yoshimasa (1436–90). He was the grandson of the founder of the Golden Pavilion, and in both cases the pavilions were part of huge retirement estates. Both became important centers of culture, and both were converted into Zen temples on the death of the owner. But whereas the Golden Pavilion is golden, the Silver Pavilion is not silver. How come?

The two-storey pavilion, which houses religious statuary, is made of plain wood. The standard explanation is that Yoshimasa ran out of money, or that he died before the project could be completed. Recent research suggests another answer, however. Yoshimasa was a devotee of moon-viewing and his most famous poem extols the pleasure of anticipation:

My lodge lies at the foot
Of the Moon-Awaiting Hill –
The shortening hill shadow
As it finally disappears
Almost fills me with regret.

The custom of the time was to hold moon-viewing parties at which saké drinking was combined with poetry writing. As the full moon was a Buddhist symbol of enlightenment, there was a spiritual dimension to the occasion, and it is thought that after gathering on the ground floor to watch the moon rise, guests would move to the second floor to look down at its reflection in the adjacent pond (indirectness being cherished in

Japanese aesthetics). The 'silverness' of the pavilion may therefore have involved moonlight reflecting onto its lacquered wood.

Garden Skills

Yoshimasa modeled his estate on Saiho-ji, with a pond garden above which an upper garden provides an overview. Appreciation of the aesthetics begins with the approach. Inside the entrance gate the path makes a sharp right turn into a long avenue lined by a tall hedge. By restricting the vision, the path focusses attention on what is to come—a first glimpse of the central dry landscape garden seen through a specially made opening.

Opposite top Raking sand or gravel into patterns, known as *samon*, takes practice to perfect. As with paintings, enormous care is taken with the 'brushstrokes' and the creations are given the same status as works of art.
Left The Silver Pavilion was modeled after that at Kinkaku-ji, although it only has two rather than three storeys. The first floor, called the Shinkudan (Empty-heart Hall), contains 1,000 images of Jizo, guardian of the afterlife. The second floor is dedicated to Kannon, deity of compassion. Although Yoshimasa practiced Zen, he also believed in Amida's Pure Land.
Above The two-meter-high Kogetsudai (Moon-viewing Platform) is thought to be a later addition to the dry garden. The base is swept every morning and the entire form remade every month. Some see it as Mt Fuji, others as the Buddhist Mt Sumeru.
Below The arrangements of nature complement those of humans in the creation of garden beauty. Irregularity of form was accordingly incorporated into Japanese aesthetics.

Inside, a raised bed of raked sand (named the Sea of Silvery Sand) is rippled so as to suggest water. Next to it stands a conical pile of sand, which was a later addition. Some see it as Mt Fuji, others as mythical Mt Sumeru, but officially it is the Moon-Viewing Platform. It stands as an upright yang complementing the horizontal yin of the sand-sea.

Next to the dry landscape is a pond with a busy microcosm of bridges, waterfall and plants. The various rocks were sent as gifts from feudal lords across Japan, each with its own individual history. It is said that Yoshimasa personally supervised the positioning of the garden features and

references to famous Japanese and Chinese scenes would have enabled him to explain them to guests on leisurely perambulations.

Building Heritage

From the pond the path leads up the adjoining hill to a spring where Yoshimasa drew water for tea ceremonies. There are vantage points over the temple grounds and city beyond, before the path leads back past a bamboo grove and moss garden with semi-rural feel. Only at the end does one approach the Silver Pavilion (an instance of the Japanese preference for indirectness). The residential style of the first floor blends with the Zen style of the second, topped by a shingled roof of Japanese cypress.

The pavilion is not the only building of interest. The Main Hall, which is open in spring and autumn, has *fusuma* paintings by celebrated painters like Yosa Buson (1716–84) and Ike no Taiga (1723–76). Here one can lose oneself in images of bamboo groves where Daoist sages enjoy drinking and playing chess. For a modern touch, there are startling nature scenes by Okuda Genso (1912–2003) covering the sliding doors of Roseitei (built for incense smelling).

The Togudo, which constituted the private quarters of Yoshimasa, is the only original structure apart from the pavilion. The paper window, tatami and alcove with staggered shelving were prototypes of the *shoin-zukuri* style, which became standard throughout Japan. It also contains the first known dedicated space for the tea ceremony. Such is the historical significance of the building that people fly across the world to study it.

The estate became the center of a flourishing 'Higashiyama Culture', which as well as the tea ceremony included flower arrangement, Noh theater, garden design, black ink painting (*sumi-e*) and incense smelling. The pursuits were heavily influenced by Buddhism, Zen in particular, and through the cultivation of *wabi* (rustic simplicity) and *yugen* (elegant profundity), the artists gathered around Yoshimasa imbued their practice with a spiritual resonance. In so doing, they perfected the arts and crafts with which we are familiar today. Ginkaku-ji is thus more than a display of Japanese aesthetics at its finest. In the words of Donald Keene, it is "the soul of Japan".

The Stroll Garden takes the visitor through a variety of landscapes, which include a moss-covered area adjacent to a bamboo grove. Moss thrives in Kyoto's moist atmosphere, and water is omnipresent through the numerous streams and underground reserves (thought to be equal in volume to Lake Biwa).

Above The deeply furrowed Sea of Silver Sand is a dry garden counterpart to a pond garden, demonstrating the Zen propensity for unifying opposites. It is shaped after China's West Lake and designed to bask in the lustrous gleam of moonlight (sadly the temple is closed in the evenings).

Below right The Togudo is not only the country's oldest *shoin*-style building but the origin of the modern tea room. Now a National Treasure, it was once Yoshimitsu's residence and stood at the heart of the thriving Higashiyama Culture. Together with the pavilion, it has survived from the original estate of those heady days.

Above Garden waterfalls can be minimalist in nature, more a trickle than a cascade. The mere suggestion is sufficient for the imagination to fill in. Sound plays a vital role, and here at the Sengetsu-sei (Moon-viewing Spring) a rock is carefully positioned to create the right auditory effect.

GINKAKU-JI AT A GLANCE

Founded 1490 when Ashikaga Yoshimasa's villa was converted into a temple. 'Temple of the Silver Pavilion' (official name Jisho-ji)

Affiliation Shokoku-ji School of Rinzai Zen

Special features Dry landscape, pond garden, pavilion, artwork, hillside views

Opening 8.30 am–5 pm; 9 am–4.30 pm Dec–Feb (¥500)

Event Special opening of buildings: spring (March–Golden Week) and autumn (Oct–Nov)

Access Bus 5, 17, 100 to Ginkaku-ji mae or 30 mins walk from Nanzen-ji along Philosopher's Walk

Contact (075) 771-5725

RYOAN-JI 竜安寺
World Famous Rock Garden
FOUNDED 1450

It is the world's most famous rock garden and the most photographed. Raked gravel, moss and rocks are bordered by walls showing the patina of age. Nothing could be simpler and yet the arrangement has proved endlessly fascinating, as if here within the narrow courtyard is compressed all the essence of Zen. Experts the world over have waxed lyrical about its appeal. Some ascribe symbolic meaning to the composition, while others insist on seeing it purely for itself. Those who have spent hours pondering the garden talk of a profound emotional response, as if the layout connects with patterns in the brain.

There are fifteen rocks in all, and interpretations have included mountain peaks protruding above cloud, islands in a cosmic ocean and a Chinese riddle about tiger cubs. The contrasting shapes suggest yin–yang significance, while the groupings of seven, five and three are important numbers for Daoism. Significantly, not all the rocks can be seen at once, which raises the notion of completeness, for in terms of the lunar cycle fifteen signifies the full moon (a Buddhist symbol of enlightenment). The implication is that the 'full picture' cannot be seen, only by those who are enlightened.

There is more to Ryoan-ji, however, than its rock garden. The Abbot's Quarters, which stand alongside, have a set of six rooms containing *fusuma* paintings, including some dramatic dragons. At the rear is a replica of the temple's famous water basin, which bears an inscription that can be read sideways as well as downwards. Learning should be for its own sake, it states, not for profit or gain.

The spacious grounds contain an attractive pond garden, popular in autumn for the changing colors.

Right The famous rock garden is framed by an attractive *wabi-sabi* wall stained by natural oils seeping out, behind which rises an assortment of flowering and non-flowering trees. The combination of three rocks, one prominent and two smaller, is suggestive of the Buddhist triad in which an enlightened being is attended by two Bodhi-sattva. It calls to mind also the Daoist triad of heaven, earth and human.

Opposite The Kyoyochi 'mirror pond', dating back to the twelfth century, is surrounded by cherry, pine and camellia trees that were brought from Korea in the Momoyama period. In June the edges of the pond are colored with iris. A shrine dedicated to Benten (muse of music and creativity) stands on a small island, and the nearby restaurant Seigen-in is dedicated to tofu (tel. 075-462-4742).

Below The north garden hosts a famous wash basin with Chinese characters that cleverly read downwards as well as crossways. The middle square (containing water) represents *kuchi*, or mouth. The inscription has been interpreted as "Learn only satisfaction," in other words, be content with what you have.

Left Although visitors focus on the famous rock garden, the temple grounds have much to offer. The pond was originally part of a Heian-era estate and the route around it has vantage points to admire the views, including that of Seven Imperial Tombs to the north, behind the Abbot's Quarters.

The moss-covered approach can be strikingly beautiful, particularly after rain, and there is a tofu restaurant with traditional atmosphere (Seigen-in, reservations 075-462-4742). The route around the pond deliberately obscures sight of the water for most part, occasionally revealing strategically placed vantage points. The prime spot looks north towards the hill behind the rock garden where lie the tombs of emperors.

The pond was originally part of an aristocratic estate dating back to Heian times. It was remodeled for the powerful warlord Hosokawa Katsumoto, who was a key figure in the Onin War (1467–77). Following his death, the buildings were converted into a Zen temple. Around 1500, the famous rock garden was added, possibly designed by the artist Soami (1472–1525). Although the temple was destroyed in a devastating fire in the 1790s, the garden survived untouched. Until the 1930s it remained relatively obscure, simply one of Kyoto's many dry landscapes. Now it is in a class of its own. Just fifteen rocks—but what an impact!

The rock garden is in the style of *hira-niwa*, or flat garden, since it rests on a level plane without mounds, trees or plants. The covering of snow makes it even more difficult to see all of the garden's fifteen rocks (fifteen signifying completion or perfection).

RYOAN-JI AT A GLANCE

Founded 1450 conversion of an estate by Giten Gensho, abbot of Myoshin-ji. 'Temple of Dragon Beneficence' (taken from the name of a Chinese mountain)

Affiliation Myoshin-ji School of Rinzai Zen

Special features Dry landscape with 15 rocks, Abbot's Quarters, pond garden

Opening 8 am–5 pm Mar–Nov; 8.30 am–4.30 pm Dec–Feb (¥500)

Access Bus to Ritsumeikan Daigaku-mae, 7 min walk or 20 min walk from Kinkaku-ji

Contact (075) 463-2216 (www.ryoanji.jp/smph/eng/)

SHUON-AN (IKKYU-JI)

酬恩庵

Ikkyu's Retirement Home

FOUNDED 1456 (ON AN EARLIER SITE)

Popularly known as Ikkyu-ji, the temple of Shuon-an is these days a homage to Japan's best-loved Zen master, Ikkyu Sojun (1394–1481). There are statues, memorabilia and a mausoleum built to his own specifications. There is even a bitter-tasting *natto* (fermented bean) on sale, made to a recipe concocted by Ikkyu. The temple, which is run now by a father and son pair of priests, has attractive grounds and Tang-style buildings with immaculate cypress bark roofs. There is also a pond garden with splendidly comic statues of *arhat* (enlightened beings). Put this all together with paintings by celebrated artist Kano Tanyu (1602–74), and the temple is well worth visiting. For admirers of Ikkyu, it is an absolute must.

The Zen master was a great admirer of Daio Kokushi, founder of Daitoku-ji, whose thirteenth-century temple on this site had fallen into ruins. To honor his predecessor, Ikkyu took charge of the rebuilding and for the latter part of his life made it his home. He was so attached to it that even after being made abbot of Daitoku-ji at the age of eighty-one, he preferred to live here and commute the long distance to Kyoto by palanquin. He died at eighty-eight, supposedly while doing *zazen*.

The highlight of the temple is a wooden statue of Ikkyu enshrined within the Hojo (Abbot's Quarters), on the very spot where he had his residence. It was created by his disciple Bokusai, and the hair used for the scalp and face were Ikkyu's own. The altar room boasts black ink paintings of Chinese scenes by the seventeenth-century genius Tanyu, and in front of the building is a simple dry landscape of raked gravel. At the back is a dry landscape in a compact space, with 'a waterfall' seeming to pour out from rugged rocks representing steep mountains and valleys.

Above A meditative moment on the wide veranda of the Main Hall. The immaculately raked sea of white gravel is given a shoreline of manicured azalea shrubs that bloom from May through early June. Gravel is often preferred to sand in raked gardens because it is less likely to be disturbed or blown away.
Right As well as being attractive ground cover, moss gives a garden the appearance of age. Kyoto's humid climate suits the plant, which is able to absorb moisture and nutrients from the air. It favors undisturbed spots such as the base of trees. Getting it to spread over wider areas takes care and loving attention.

The Founder's Hall houses a statue of Daio Kokushi, and in the grounds beyond is a statue of the young Ikkyu sweeping leaves (the head is shiny from where people have stroked it in the hope of absorbing his quick wit). The Treasury has a portrait of him by Soga Dosaku, above which is a piece of calligraphy by Ikkyu himself saying "Ikkyu alone has received the teaching transmitted by Rinzai." The museum also boasts Ikkyu's last will. For tea enthusiasts, there is the Kokyu-an Tea Ceremony House (which requires advance application). It has a dry landscape attributed to his disciple Murata Shuko. Next to it stands Ikkyu's mausoleum, which is not under the auspices of the temple but of the Imperial Household Agency, for the

'wild man of Zen' is presumed to have been the illegitimate son of Emperor Go-Komatsu. In death, as in life, Ikkyu continues to be exceptional.

At the back of the Main Hall is a small Horai garden in which the mythical mountain is represented by the rock in the upper right corner from which other elements seem to flow. Here in the Isles of the Blessed dwelt Daoist Immortals, who had managed to transcend the dualities of life.

SHUON-AN AT A GLANCE

Founded 13 c as Myosho-ji by Daio Kokushi; 1456 refounded as Shuon-an by Ikkyu. 'Hermitage of Repaying Indebtedness' (to the Buddha)

Affiliation Daitoku-ji School of Rinzai Zen

Special features Ikkyu's memorabilia, Abbot's Quarters, pond garden, *shojin ryori* bento (from ¥1850; reserve two days in advance)

Opening 9 am–5 pm; Treasury House 9.30 am–4.30 pm (¥500)

Event Last Sun of Jan: Ikkyu Zenzai (memorial with sweet red bean soup); mid-Sept: Ikkyu-ji Takigi Noh (torchlight play)

Access 30 mins by train to Shintanabe (Kintetsu) or Kyotanabe (JR), then 20 mins walk

Contact 0774-62-0193 (www.ikkyuji.org/en/)

IKKYU SOJUN (1394-1481)

The eccentric Ikkyu is Japan's favorite Zen monk, a folk hero celebrated in manga and anime for being direct and speaking from the heart. He had harsh words for fellow monks whom he suspected of being more interested in worldly success than spiritual merit. Meanwhile, he himself openly drank alcohol and frequented brothels. For much of his life, he wandered around Kansai living rough, yet in addition to expertise in tea he was a gifted calligrapher, artist and flautist, whose circle of admirers included the leading figures of the day. For R. H. Blyth, he was simply "the greatest Zen monk in Japan."

Ikkyu was just five when his mother fell into disfavor and he was sent for training to the Kyoto temple of Ankoku-ji. Word got around that he was a child prodigy and the shogun Ashikaga Yoshimitsu went to visit him. Seeing a painting of a tiger amidst bamboo, Yoshimitsu asked the young boy to catch it for him. "Only if you drive it out first," was the response.

At thirteen Ikkyu entered Kennin-ji, but left because of its laxness to study with a master called Keno, who became a sort of father figure. When Keno died, Ikkyu tried to commit suicide. Before long he found another master called Kaso, who had a reputation for strictness, and stayed with him for nine years. It was from Kaso that he received his name (*ikkyu* means 'one pause').

From the world of passions
Returning to the world beyond passions
There's but a moment's pause

In 1420, Ikkyu was enlightened when he heard a crow caw while meditating in a boat on Lake Biwa. After he received the certification (*inka shomei*), he tore it up as meaningless. Rather than a piece of paper, authenticity mattered to him. Between the ages of twenty-nine and fifty-seven Ikkyu took to a wandering life, dubbing himself Crazy Cloud and writing poems that were acerbic and personal.

A Crazy Cloud, out in the open
Blown about madly, as wild as they come
Who knows where this cloud will go,
Where the wind will still?

Anecdotes abound about Ikkyu. When invited to a ceremony at Daitoku-ji, he turned up in rags, and after bering reprimanded he angrily questioned whether the invitation had been for him or for his clothes. Every New Year's Day he would carry around a stick with a skull on top. "Each time we greet the New Year, we take a step towards death," he warned passers-by. He was also known to carry around a wooden sword and when questioned about it he would explain that it was fake, just like the Zen of the large monasteries.

In his seventies, Ikkyu fell in love with a blind woman some forty years his junior and he wrote touching poems about the affair:

The trees wither, the leaves fall,
But spring comes round again.
Greenery grows, flowers bloom,
And old promises are renewed.
Mori, should I forget my deep gratitude
Let me be reborn a beast for all eternity.

In later life he led the restoration of Daitoku-ji by bullying the merchants of Sakai for donations. Meanwhile, he lived on at Shuon-an as the revered elder statesman of Zen, preparing for death by erecting his own mausoleum. His parting instructions show he retained his fierce independence to the end: "After my death, there will be those who will go to the forests or mountains [to meditate], and some may drink saké or enjoy women, but those disciples who lecture to an audience for money, talking about Zen as 'the moral way', these men misappropriate Buddhism and are, in reality, Ikkyu's enemies."

A statue of Ikkyu.

ENKO-JI 圓光寺

Spacious Grounds with a Prized Garden

FOUNDED 1601

Enko-ji is popular in autumn because of the beauty of its maple-filled garden. Otherwise the temple is largely overlooked although it has much to offer: spacious grounds, a quiet atmosphere, famous artwork, dry landscape, bamboo grove and fine views. Moreover, it is just a few minutes from the popular Shisendo hermitage. The temple is concerned to preserve a religious atmosphere as the neat rows of *zabuton* meditation cushions in the Zendo attest. "Enko-ji teaches listening to one's inner voice and seeking truth," says the genial priest Keikan Otsubo.

The temple was originally located in Fushimi, where it was founded as an education center. It moved to the present site in 1667 and played an important part in disseminating Buddhism in its 'Enko-ji editions', printed with imported wooden type. Samples are displayed in a small exhibit room, one side of which is taken up by a magnificent folding screen of bamboo by Maruyama Okyo (1733–95); the artist was fond of the temple's bamboo grove. In front of the building is an unusual dry garden of raked sand representing a white dragon swirling between upright splinters of rock.

The Main Hall contains Chinese ink landscape paintings by Tomioka Tessai (1837–1924), which convey the idea of immersion in nature. To one side are displayed contemporary Rimpa School paintings that with their brash colors seem quite at odds with the subdued tones associated with Zen. But for most people the main 'artwork' is the garden. The verdant mix of moss, azalea, rock and pond is a perfect illustration of the harmony with nature for which Japanese gardens are famous, lulling the observer into meditative reverie. The autumn illumination here had a high reputation for the stunning lighting of the maple trees but the temple recently stopped the practice for fear of the damage it might be causing.

Surprisingly, at the back of the temple is a grave for Tokugawa Ieyasu, who is famously buried at Nikko. (On enquiry, it turns out that the grave

Honryu-tei (Running Dragon Garden) is a daring depiction of a dragon about to take flight in a sea of clouds. To the left of the picture is the head with two upright rocks for horns. Other rocks indicate the coiled snake-like body sticking out of the clouds, with flashes of lightning represented by the tall vertical rocks in moss.

contains one of his teeth.) From the small hill is a view over temple grounds and a portion of the city beyond.

A special feature of the temple is a *suikinkutsu* (auditory chamber) beneath a wash basin near the Main Hall. As the water drips from above, it echoes in an underground pot, giving off a distinctive sound. This was intended to accompany the washing of hands on the way to tea ceremonies, acting as a form of spiritual purification. Listen carefully, and in the sound of a single drop falling to oblivion can be heard the merging of one with the infinite.

The inner garden shows delicate patterns of bamboo and maple. One person to be inspired by such scenes was the artist Maruyama Okyo, a frequent visitor to the temple whose painted screens can be viewed in the temple museum.

ENKO-JI AT A GLANCE

Founded 1601 by Tokugawa Ieyasu; founding priest Genkitsu Sanyo (Kanshitsu). 'Temple of the Perfect Radiance'

Affiliation Nanzen-ji School of Rinzai Zen

Special features Artwork, garden, large grounds, *suikinkutsu* sound effect

Opening 9 am–5 pm (¥500)

Zazen Sun 6–8 am (Dec–Feb 7–9 am), short talk, rice (¥1000); by reservation

Event Viewing maple colors: 7–8 am (¥1000); reserve a day before

Access Eizan Railway to Shugakuin or Ichijoji, walk 15 mins; bus 5 to Ichijoji Sagarimatsucho, walk 7 mins

Contact (075) 781-8025

SHISENDO 詩仙堂

Hermitage for a Former Warrior

FOUNDED 1641

The entrance to Jozan's hermitage is a rustic gateway that speaks of humility as much as privacy. The former warrior designed his retreat when he was fifty-nine years old, enjoying a long retirement devoted to poetry, tea and Confucianism.

Shisendo is a favorite with lovers of Kyoto because of the aesthetics and sense of seclusion. It would once have stood outside the capital in rural surrounds, and something of the atmosphere still remains, lending the setting a certain charm. The founder, Ishikawa Jozan (1583–1672), was a samurai long in the service of Tokugawa Ieyasu, but the pair fell out over strategy. A lover of the arts, Ishikawa took orders at Myoshin-ji, and when he was nearly sixty built a hermitage in the manner of Confucian literati. He named it after a set of *Thirty-Six Chinese Poets*, whose portraits by master artist Kano Tanyu (1602–74) line the study. Here he practiced poetry, garden design, tea and calligraphy.

Jozan had no children, and following his death the villa was converted to a temple, passing in mid-Edo times into the care of the Soto sect. The priests put in charge adopted the Ishikawa name and the present incumbent, who lives in a house opposite, is the 14th in succession. As a result, and unusually for Kyoto, Shisendo offers Soto-style *zazen* for lay people.

The small estate is a model of Japanese aesthetics, beginning with the low rustic entrance gate. Although not robust enough to prevent access, it serves a purpose by compelling the visitor to bow on entering. Only at the inner gate is the visitor granted a view of the thatched main building with its

The white sand and trimmed azalea bushes provide a peaceful scene which extends into a background of trees and surrounding hillside. The garden descends in tiers, with the lower portion being added after World War II and affording views over Kyoto.

SHISENDO AT A GLANCE

Founded 1641 as a villa for retired samurai Ishikawa Jozan. 'Hall of the Immortal Poets'
Affiliation Eihei-ji School of Soto Zen (official name Jozan-ji)
Special features Hermitage and garden
Opening 9 am–5 pm (¥500)
Zazen 1st/3rd Sunday 6–8 am: free trial period (¥3000 per annum)
Event May 25–27: display of Jozan's portrait and calligraphy, azaleas in bloom
Access Bus no. 5 to Ichijoji Sagarimatsucho, 5 mins walk
Contact (075) 781-2954 (www.kyoto-shisendo.com/En)

upper floor moon-viewing room. Through open sliding screens comes a dazzling glimpse of the bright greenery beyond.

Inside the building is an altar room and study room, though visitors tend to gravitate to the veranda looking onto the garden. Here people sit immersed in—and entranced by—the view before them. An area of brushed white sand is bordered by a line of undulating azalea bushes, behind which a backdrop of trees merges into the 'borrowed scenery' of the nearby hills. The visual composition is accompanied by the soothing soundscape of a small waterfall and the clacking of a deer scarer (*shishi-odoshi*). (It was the first ornamental use of the farmer's device of bamboo and stone.)

It is possible to stroll around the lower portions of the garden added after World War II, which have over a hundred different plants. There is a small pond, a tea room and views over northern Kyoto. However, it is the meditative view from the veranda that makes Shisendo so special, for interior and exterior merge seamlessly into each other. The aging Jozan would have sat here, surrounded by his beloved poets and luxuriating in his own private patch of paradise. Here, indeed, it is possible to truly feel "at one with the world".

Top There are over a hundred species of plants in the garden. Here fallen maple leaves stick to wet peony leaves after an autumn shower.
Middle Lacecap hydrangea blooms in early June and is associated with the rainy season.
Bottom The repeated clack of the 'deer scarer' (*shishi-odoshi*) is a notable feature of the garden. It is uncertain whether Jozan intended it to scare away wild animals or to add a rustic note, but it is the first recorded use of the device for garden purposes.

MANPUKU-JI 萬福寺
Head Temple of the Obaku Sect

FOUNDED 1661

Manpuku-ji is unique among Kyoto's Zen temples. The architecture is different, the clothing different, the statues radically different from elsewhere. Established in 1661 by an immigrant monk, it has retained its Chinese Ming character into the present day. This is nowhere more evident than in the statuary, exemplified by a large pot-bellied Hotei (considered a manifestation of Amida). The distinctiveness runs throughout the temple—even the food and the chanting of sutra are markedly Chinese in character.

In 1639, Japan closed itself off from the outside world, with exceptions made for the Dutch at Dejima and the Chinese community in Nagasaki. The latter invited a sixty-five year old monk from China, Yinguan Longqi (later Ingen Ryuki, 1592–1673) to introduce his teaching to Japan. In 1654 he arrived with twenty disciples and a host of craftsmen. Four years later, he won the backing of the Tokugawa shogunate and obtained land for a temple at Uji, just outside Kyoto. At the time, Neo-Confucianism was in style and Buddhism was suffering

from corruption and malaise. Thanks to Ingen, the new style of Zen acted as a reinvigorating force and was supported by influential figures like retired emperor Go-Mizunoo.

The new temple took its name from Ingen's Chinese monastery. He saw himself as part of the Rinzai tradition, since he could trace his lineage back to the founder, Linji (Rinzai). However, he encountered resistance from the Japanese authorities because of the differences in style. Ingen used a different form of ordination, embraced elements of Pure Land belief and kept to the Chinese style in such aspects as clothing and eating from a communal bowl. One distinctive practice was recital of the *nembutsu* (belief in Amida) while pondering the *koan* "Who is chanting?" Excluded by the Rinzai sect, Manpuku-ji followers founded their own Obaku sect.

The first thirteen abbots of the temple were all Chinese immigrants, meaning that Manpuku-ji continued to act as a conduit for continental ideas. It stimulated fresh developments in fields such as sculpture, medicine, publishing, diet, calligraphy and painting. (Interestingly, even Western perspectives in art, which had been adopted in China, passed through Manpuku-ji to influence painters such as Ike no Taiga (1723–76).) The new Ming style is evident in *chinzo* portraiture, in one of which Ingen is depicted against a landscape given a sense of depth through shading and coloration.

A notable innovation was a tea ceremony based on *sencha* leaves rather than *matcha* powder. The ritual, which involves steeping the leaves in a small pot of hot water, was popularized by an eighteenth-century monk named Baisao ('the old tea seller'), who is commemorated in a hall named after him. Next to it are the headquarters of the Sencha Association, which every May organizes the largest tea gathering in Japan.

Left The Buddha Hall in the morning light. Manpuku-ji has twenty-three buildings in all and the distinctive Ming style of architecture marks them out from Kyoto's other Zen temples.
Above Most of the buildings are linked by long covered corridors that are hung with Chinese-style lanterns. The pine trees beyond are wrapped with straw to protect them by fooling pests into laying their eggs there.
Below The distinctive paths of diamond-shaped stepping stones are said to represent the scales on the belly of a dragon.

Shutters open onto a circular window, Buddhist symbol of enlightenment and a reminder to the monks of their daily struggle for perfection.

Temple Precincts

Visitors can wander freely around the precincts
to admire the twenty-three distinctive Ming-style
buildings. The richly hued wood is imported teak
from China and Thailand. The temple's main
object of worship is a seated Shakyamuni (Gautama
Buddha), and there are striking sculptures of *arhat*
by the Chinese artist Han Dosei. Latticed balu-
strades have Buddhist swastika patterning, and a
wooden board struck each day at dawn bears an
inscription of the accompanying chant:

> All you who practice the Way,
> Pay heed: birth and death are the
>   one great matter.
> Nothing is permanent, time moves on.
> Awake! Devote yourselves to
>   training and do not waste time.

The Bunkaden (Museum), open in spring and
autumn, has a realistic figure of Ingen at age
eighty with wrinkles and fine white hair, which is
displayed in spring and autumn. The temple also
boasts a complete set of Buddhist scriptures
painstakingly completed in 1678 after seventeen
years' work. It involved 60,000 printing blocks
(still in use) and was funded by donations
collected from throughout the entire country.

Today, there are some twenty priests attached
to the temple (three in training at the time of
writing), the vast majority of whom are hereditary.
Because of the location, it is relatively quiet except
for the bus loads of tourists who arrive for the
lunch of *fucha ryori*. The vegetarian food was
developed for ceremonies and has a Chinese
touch, which differentiates it from the standard
Zen-style *shojin ryori*. Here, the temple pamphlet
says, you get "a true taste of the Zen mind". (There
are two restaurants, one of which is within the
temple and requires three days' advance reservation. For Hakuun-an just outside, it is also best
to call beforehand (tel. 0774-31-8017).

Ingen Ryuki (1592–1673)

Ingen Ryuki started life as Yinyuan Longqi, a poor Chinese boy
whose father set out on a trip from which he never returned.
The young boy supported his family as best he could by
farming and woodcutting, then once an adult he set out in
search of his father. One night he stayed at a temple and
had a visionary realization that the Kannon bodhisattva
there was a manifestation of his father. Following the death
of his mother, he joined the local Wanfu Temple, where he
led the reconstruction project after it burnt down, and later
served as abbot.

Ingen was already sixty-five when an invitation came from
the Chinese community at Nagasaki to introduce his teaching
to Japan. It was a time of turmoil in China following the fall of
the Ming Dynasty, and Ingen took the opportunity to leave the
country. As well as introducing new aspects of Chinese culture
to Japan, Ingen wrote many books and was a key figure in the
revitalization of Zen.

By the time of Ingen's death, there were twenty-four Obaku
temples, and for his work he was awarded the posthumous
title of Daiko Fusho Kokushi (Great Teacher). He is credited
with introducing *udon* and the use of *mokugyo* drums. To
modern Japanese, his name remains familiar through the
Ingen bean, once a precious source of protein in the monastic
diet but now widely available in supermarkets. In this and so
many ways, the influential monk from Ming China could truly
be said to have left a legacy of Ten Thousand-fold Happiness.

Below The Somon outer gate has upright corner tiles depicting *makara*, imaginary creatures of Indian folklore that are half aquatic and half terrestrial. They were adopted as tile ornaments by the Obaku Sect, adding a distinctive twist to the roofline.

Above One of Manpuku-ji's main figures of worship is Hotei, known in China as the Laughing Buddha or the Fat Buddha. He is thought to have originated as a Chinese master who became identified with an incarnation of Maitreya, Buddha of the Future.
Below The distinctive railings on the stone corridor to the Founder's Hall display the auspicious Buddhist swastika, symbol of good fortune.

MANPUKU-JI AT A GLANCE

Founded 1661 by Ingen (Chinese, Yinyuan Longqi). 'Temple of Ten Thousand-fold Happiness'

Affiliation Head temple of Obaku Zen (10 subtemples, 460 branch temples)

Special features Chinese art and architecture, *fucha ryori* lunch (from ¥3200)

Opening 9 am–4.30 pm (¥500)

Zazen Available in the Hatto, ring to arrange (¥1000); also sutra copying

Event 16th each month, *sencha* ceremony, 11 am; April 3: Ingen memorial; May, middle weekend: *sencha* gathering (¥5500, reservation); early Oct: moon-viewing and tea (¥3000, reservation)

Access 5 mins walk from Obaku Station, Keihan or JR lines

Contact (0774) 32-3900 (zen.rinnou.net)

KANGA-AN 閑臥庵
A Sublime Taste of Zen

FOUNDED 1671

View of the entrance path from inside the main hall.

Imagine a tatami room overlooking an illuminated dry landscape garden. Bushes, buildings and maple trees are discretely lit, and the plaintive notes of a *shakuhachi* flute provide background ambience. A *tokonoma* alcove displays a hanging scroll of a splendid cockerel by Ito Jakuchu (1716–1800), beneath which is a small statue of Kannon, deity of compassion, astride a cow. On the table is a selection of mouth-watering delicacies, such as lotus root in vinegar dressing, aubergine with miso, sesame tofu, green tea *somen* and sweet and sour skimmed tofu.

After the meal you have a drink in the elegant bar, which is housed in what used to be the private quarters of the abbot. Now the temple is headed by a nun and the catering carried out by lay assistants. The opportunity to drink and dine in authentic Zen surroundings is the sort of thing for which people fly across the world, yet Kanga-an remains surprisingly low key.

The temple was founded when retired Emperor Go-Mizunoo asked the abbot of Manpuku-ji for protection of the northern side of the Imperial Palace (the northeast was believed particularly vulnerable to evil spirits). An unusual deity named Chintakurefushin (Holy Spirit of Residential Protection) was installed as one of the objects of worship. In 1868, when Emperor Meiji left Kyoto to reside in Tokyo, the temple lost its *raison d'etre*. It also lost its financial support. Thirty years ago, it turned to serving the Obaku style of vegan food of which Go-Mizunoo was so fond. Known as *fucha ryori*, it enhances the plain food of monks with the elegance of court cuisine and a Chinese touch.

Kanga-an is the only member of the Obaku sect in Kyoto (the head temple of Manpuku-ji is in the city of Uji). Daytime visitors can enjoy the *arhat* statues at the entrance and the Worship Hall, followed by a green tea set overlooking the garden. It is the evenings, however, which make Kanga-an so unusual, for lanterns line the path and illumined buildings appear like a vision against the night sky. When you put this together with the food, you may feel that Kanga-an is indeed unique in more than one sense.

KANGA-AN AT A GLANCE

Founded 1671 by retired Emperor Go-Mizunoo; founding priest Sengai. 'Hermitage of Quiet Rest'

Affiliation Obaku Sect

Special features Vegetarian *fucha ryori*, evening illumination

Opening 1–10 pm (¥500); green tea set (¥500). Reserve for meals in advance: lunch (¥5000); dinner (from ¥8000); bar (¥1000 cover charge)

Event Aug 16: Memorial and dinner for past emperors (¥10,000); reserve in advance

Access Kuramaguchi subway station exit 1, then 2 mins walk

Contact (075) 256-2480

Top The pinkish color of the sesame tofu is made from cherry extract. The seasonal touch is part of a presentation meant to appeal to the eye as much as the mouth.
Above left Kanga-an's bar looks out onto a rear garden which takes on a fairytale atmosphere when illuminated at night.
Left The elegant interiors of Kanga-an feature *fusuma* sliding screens decorated with gold and silver foil, which reflect enough light that electric lighting is unnecessary during the day. The graceful floor lamps are made from single sheets of Japanese paper.

Maples are a popular item in Japanese gardens for their finely shaped leaves add grace, beauty and color. They also act as intermediary between ground bushes and the dizzying height of cedars.

ENTSU-JI 円通寺

A Celebrated 'Borrowed Scenery' Garden

FOUNDED 1678

Entsu-ji is not easily accessible, which is good news for those looking to escape the bustling crowds of downtown Kyoto. The peace of the temple is just what is needed to appreciate its celebrated main feature—a garden with the 'borrowed scenery' of Mt Hiei. The mountain played a vital role in Japanese history, for it was from its heights that emerged the great founding figures of Japanese Buddhism. They include Myoan Eisai (1141–1215) and Eihei Dogen (1200–53), the founders of Rinzai and Soto Zen, who both studied on Mt Hiei before leaving to follow a different path.

The temple owes its existence to the relative coolness of the location, for the area was a summer resort for Kyoto aristocrats. Retired Emperor Go-Mizunoo (1596–1680) provides an example, for he created a small retreat here after being frustrated in his ambitions by the power of the shogunate. Twenty years later, when he completed the much grander Shugakuin, his old villa was converted to a temple. It enjoyed *monzeki* status (temples to which priests of aristo-cratic lineage were appointed). This makes it different from a family temple, and the present priest likes to point out that his job is not hereditary but awarded on merit.

The temple has few items of note, although the eleventh-century Kannon housed in the altar is by the renowned sculptor Jocho Busshi (d. 1057). The Study Room was a gift from the Imperial Palace, and the twentieth-century paintings in the Main Hall were by an artist allowed to use the temple for his convalescence. However, the whole focus of the temple is on its borrowed scenery and there is ample space for viewing from the Main Hall.

The original garden, attributed variously to Kobori Enshu or Go-Mizunoo, fell into disrepair and was restored after World War II. Enclosed by an immaculately trimmed hedge of azaleas and camellias, it contains some forty moss-covered rocks. 'Borrowed

scenery' is often used mistakenly to simply denote a scenic backdrop, but the technique involves the conscious integration of a remote feature into the garden composition. Here at Entsu-ji the eye is drawn upwards from the rock garden by vigorous cedar trunks, while the layered effect of manicured hedge in the foreground together with dishevelled bamboo in the middle distance draw in the contours of the mountain beyond.

Seated in the right position, the viewer sees Mt Hiei perfectly framed by bush, tree and foliage. Sometimes misty, sometimes startlingly clear, the mountain changes its appearance not only by season but even during the course of a single day. If the conditions are right, the sole accompaniment will be birdsong and the sensuous touch of the breeze. The pathos of life's transient beauty is rarely so evident, yet the delicacy of this carefully crafted scene

has been encroached upon by modern development, and even threatened altogether. For the moment, 'the mother of Japanese Buddhism' continues to rise above it all, sublime and supreme. More than 1,200 years of ascetic and religious endeavor have taken place on its unforgiving heights, and it would be hard to imagine scenery that could be more appropriately 'borrowed'.

Above Mt Hiei is skillfully incorporated into the garden composition, making for Kyoto's most famous example of *shakkei*, or 'borrowed scenery'. The view is best appreciated on clear, crisp days when the mountain stands out distinctly, though moist days can have a charm of their own when misty clouds form below the peak.
Opposite below The main garden features low-lying stones amongst moss and bushes, as if a natural outcropping. The hedge, which forms the background, is kept to a carefully calculated height so as to give a sense of tiering up to the distant mountain.

ENTSU-JI AT A GLANCE

Founded Estate 1638 by Go-Mizunoo; temple 1678 by founding nun Enkoin Bunei. 'Temple of the Perfect Communion'

Affiliation Myoshin-ji School of Rinzai Zen

Special features Dry landscape with 'borrowed scenery'

Opening 10 am–4.30 pm; Dec–March 10 am–4 pm (¥500); green tea set (¥400)

Access Bus 45 to Entsuji Michi, then 10 mins walk

Contact (075) 781-1875

KONPUKU-JI 金福寺
A Temple of Poets
FOUNDED c.1686

Konpuku-ji is a small temple known for its haiku
associations. The Basho-an hut, which honors the poet
Matsuo Basho's (1644–94) stay at the temple, stands near
to the grave of another famous haiku writer, Yosa Buson
(1716–84). There is a dry landscape garden, Chinese
bellflowers and azalea bushes set on an attractive wooded
slope, but the human associations are what make this
temple special. It serves as a locus where Zen interfaces
with haiku, and in recent years the temple has established a
display room and put up explanatory boards (in Japanese).

The temple was founded in the ninth century by Ennin
(794–864), a famous Tendai abbot, but was later destroyed
and for several centuries lay in disuse. Then in the seventeenth century the priest Tesshu, head of nearby Enko-ji,
renovated the site and brought it under the auspices of
Rinzai Zen. It was his acquaintance with Basho that led
to the poet staying at a hut on the site for some days:

All night I listened
to the howling autumn wind
on the temple hill

A hundred years after Basho's time, the poet-artist Yosa
Buson came across the ruined hut and rebuilt it in homage
to the poet. The result was the two-roomed tea house we
see today, with its thatched roof of miscanthus. Here Buson
held haiku gatherings, and for a memorial service in honor
of Basho he composed a special poem:

**Straw coat, bamboo hat
convey impression of the master—
winter rainfall**

During his lifetime Buson was rated more highly as a painter than a poet, and several of his scrolls are on display at the temple as well as a portrait of Basho. Such was his affection for his predecessor that he erected a stone inscribed with Basho's haiku, and an essay he wrote about restoring the hut talks lovingly of the "deeply hidden place":

**When dead let me lie
Near the Basho monument—
Withered pampas grass**

Buson's grave lies, as he wished, near the monument to Basho, and from the small slope are views over northern Kyoto. Several of Buson's most devoted disciples chose to be buried close by. There are surprisingly few visitors here, and with its panorama and natural surrounds the spot provides a fitting setting for reflective thought. *Ars longa vita brevis.*

Above The reconstruction of Basho's dilapidated hut was carried out by Buson in homage to his predecessor. Once completed, the hut served for poetry gatherings. Buson asked to be buried nearby, and some of his followers chose to be buried alongside him.
Opposite top The gravestone of eighteenth-century haiku master Yosa Buson.
Left The lower garden with Basho-an in the background. Since Buson's time, many famous haiku poets have visited the temple and their verse is featured on boards along the slope leading to the top, from where there is a fine view over Kyoto.

KONPUKU-JI AT A GLANCE

Founded 864 on the request of Ennin; c. 1686 refounded by Tesshu. 'Temple of Golden Bliss'
Affiliation Nanzen-ji School of Rinzai Zen
Special features Basho-an thatched hut, Buson's grave, Buson portrait of Basho
Opening 9 am–5 pm (¥400)
Access Bus 5 to Ichijoji-Sagarimatsu, 10 mins walk; 5 mins from Shisendo
Contact (075) 791-1666

Published by Tuttle Publishing, an imprint of Periplus Editions (HK) Ltd

www.tuttlepublishing.com

Copyright © 2024 Periplus Editions (HK) Ltd
Page 86—Source: Wikimedia Commons

ISBN 978-4-8053-1808-9 pb
(*Previously published under ISBN 978-4-8053-1401-2 hc*)

Distributed by

North America, Latin America & Europe
Tuttle Publishing
364 Innovation Drive
North Clarendon, VT 05759-9436 U.S.A.
Tel: 1 (802) 773-8930; Fax: 1 (802) 773-6993
info@tuttlepublishing.com; www.tuttlepublishing.com

Japan
Tuttle Publishing
Yaekari Building 3rd Floor
5-4-12 Osaki Shinagawa-ku, Tokyo 141-0032
Tel: (81) 3 5437-0171; Fax: (81) 3 5437-0755
sales@tuttle.co.jp; www.tuttle.co.jp

Asia Pacific
Berkeley Books Pte. Ltd.
3 Kallang Sector, #04-01, Singapore 349278
Tel: (65) 6741-2178; Fax: (65) 6741-2179
inquiries@periplus.com.sg; www.periplus.com

Pb 26 25 24   10 9 8 7 6 5 4 3 2 1

Printed in China   2401EP

TUTTLE PUBLISHING® is a registered trademark of Tuttle Publishing, a division of Periplus Editions (HK) Ltd.

Acknowledgments and Credits

John Dougill would like to acknowledge the invaluable assistance of Yuriko Suzuki, who facilitated much of the research, and also the expertise of Thomas Kirchner, who kindly showed me around Rinsen-ji, part of the great monastical complex of Tenryu-ji. I am also very grateful to Rev. Takafumi Kawakami for making time in his busy schedule, and to novelist Julie Highmore for reading over the text. I am indebted, too, to several experts in the field. These include prominent academics such as John Nelson, George Keyworth, Robert Borgen, Hoyu Ishida and Eisho Nasu. I was also fortunate to have the support of Zen priest Tom Wright, landscape designer Tomoki Kato, Japan journalist Eric Johnston, *shakuhachi* maestro Preston Houser, *Kyoto Journal* editor Ken Rodgers, former Kyoto city official Shigenori Shibata, Kyoto author Judith Clancy, garden expert Mark Hovane, and two International Goodwill Ambassadors for the City of Kyoto, Jeff Bergland and tea master Randy Channell. Thanks also to photographer Damien Douxchamps. Finally, I would like to restate my gratitude to scholar Michel Mohr for the invaluable input he provided on a previous occasion when I wrote about Zen in Kyoto, and also for the encouragement of author Norman Waddell. My sincere thanks to one and all.

The quotation from Ruth Fuller Sasaki in the Introduction is an abridged version of an article included in *Zen Pioneer: The Life and Works of Ruth Fuller Sasaki* by Isabel Stirling, published by Shoemaker and Hoard in the US, 2006, pages 198–203. The original piece was by Ruth Fuller Sasaki for a 1960 pamphlet titled "Rinzai Zen Study for Foreigners in Japan," published privately in Kyoto by the First Zen Institute of America in Japan.

John Einarsen is extremely grateful for the help he received in taking photographs for this book. First and foremost are two Zen priests who are playing a crucial role in introducing Zen to overseas visitors: Rev. Takafumi Kawakami of Shunko-in and Rev. Daiko Matsuyama of Taizo-in. They graciously allowed me to photograph at their temples on several occasions. I especially wish to express my deep gratitude to the deputy priest of Ikkyu-ji, Soko Tanabe, who posed for some of the photographs, and to his wife who prepared tea and sweets. This encounter never would have materialized if it were not for the kind help of Kyoto photographers Hideyuki and Kayu Mizuno. I would like to thank Gensho Hozumi of Toko-ji and the International Zen Center for hosting me on several occasions, and Sage Morita Einarsen for his amazing temple compound illustration on pages 24–25. Others who helped include the many monks at the temples who answered my simple questions, Thomas Kirchner, garden designer Marc P. Keane, *Kyoto Journal*'s Ken Rodgers and Toshihiro Hagimori, who first encouraged me to do a book like this many years ago. Finally, I would like to express my appreciation to Midori Morita who accompanied me to many of the temples. She was a fun, patient and helpful companion on these trips.

"Books to Span the East and West"